ISLAND

HALIBUT FISHERMAN

ISLAND
HALIBUT FISHERMAN

by Robert H. Jones and Larry E. Stefanyk

HARBOUR PUBLISHING

Harbour Publishing Co. Ltd.
P.O. Box 219
Madeira Park, BC
V0N 2H0
www.harbourpublishing.com

Printed and bound in Canada
Text Design by Warren Clark
Cover photo credit: Janice M. Stefanyk

Harbour Publishing acknowledges financial support from the Government of
Canada through the Book Publishing Industry Development Program and the
Canada Council for the Arts, and from the Province of British Columbia
through the British Columbia Arts Council and the Book Publisher's Tax
Credit through the Ministry of Provincial Revenue.

Library and Archives Canada Cataloguing in Publication

Jones, Robert H., 1935-
    Island halibut fisherman / Robert H. Jones and Larry E. Stefanyk.
    Includes index.
ISBN 978-1-55017-414-4
    1. Pacific halibut fishing—British Columbia—Pacific Coast—
Guidebooks. I. Stefanyk, Larry E. II. Title.
SH691.H3J65 2007   799.17'6950916433   C2007-900184-X

DISCLAIMER
There is no actual or implied warranty concerning the accuracy or
suitability of the map coordinates listed in this book for any uses
whatsoever. The authors, publisher, and sources of cartographic
information expressly disclaim any responsibility for any loss or
damage resulting from the use of these coordinates or related information.

DEDICATION

To the ladies in our lives:
Janice Stefanyk with her sharp eye for cameras
and shooting beautiful photographs, and Vera Jones
with her equally sharp eye for misplaced or missing
punctuation and lapses in syntax.

ACKNOWLEDGEMENTS

Thanks to crack fishing guides Corey Hayes,
Jason Mohl, Brian Lacroix and Bill von Brendel
for their assistance during their busiest time of the season,
Robert Alcock at the Delta Tackle Company, Robert Van Pelt
at Pacific Bait & Tackle, Dan Boudreau at Gone Fishin'
in Courtenay, Tom Vaida at Island Outfitters Sportfishing
Centre in Victoria and Calvin Blood at the International Pacific
Halibut Commission in Seattle. Special thanks to Ralph Shaw
for frequently making himself available to provide odds
and ends of tackle, equipment, and assorted bits
and pieces, usually on short notice after all other
avenues had been exhausted.

TABLE OF CONTENTS

PART THREE

INTRODUCTION

. . . .

As the publisher and editor respectively of *Island Fisherman* magazine, Larry E. Stefanyk and I agree that the best part of our jobs is meeting people who share our interest in recreational fishing—freshwater and saltwater. We also agree that the inter-

est in halibut fishing has been increasing dramatically over the past few years, attracting neophytes of all ages, eager to learn, to the ranks of the wise old "high-liners" with several decades of saltwater experience. Occasionally we encounter genuine experts—people whose fishing prowess has earned the respect and admiration of others. Whenever possible we make a point of interviewing them, and these interviews provide the sort of information that could otherwise be gathered only by devoting years to being out there fishing. While it's true that most of the emphasis in our interviews has been on salmon fishing—mainly chinooks and coho—virtually all of the gurus we encounter are also dedicated halibut anglers.

Larry Stefanyk holds a West Coast halibut.

If finding an expert to interview is like striking it rich, going fishing with one is a bonanza. I have hit the mother lode on a few occasions over the years—the first time was with Ian Andersen, skipper of the *Silver Fox* out of Port Hardy, who put me onto my first halibut back in the 1980s. Ian always took great delight in waiting until all of the rod-and-reelers on board were dead

1

certain that there were absolutely no halibut "down there," whereupon he would make an elaborate production of digging out his 300-pound-test handline, dropping a 1½-pound Lucky Jig to the bottom and always—yes, always—hooking a halibut. This usually occurred within a minute or two of dunking his jig, though on a really slow day he might have to jig for up to 10 minutes.

The largest halibut I have ever watched being caught was also the fastest I have ever seen landed. Takashi Tateno and I were watching Murray Gardham, the former owner of Double Bay Resort on Hanson Island, preparing a catch of pink salmon for the hot smoker. He severed the head from the first salmon and impaled it on a large circle hook that was tied to a 400-pound-test handline. This he lowered off the dock, which was floating in scarcely 40 feet of water. Now I wasn't using a stopwatch, but in about five minutes the handline set up a commotion

Murray Gardham took scarcely six minutes to catch and land this 138-pounder on his dock.

on the deck. Murray pounced on it and started hauling on the line, yelling for someone to fetch a harpoon from a nearby boat. When a guest returned with a harpoon, Murray asked him to loop it to a dock cleat. Within about three minutes after hooking what was obviously a large fish, Murray actually had it close enough to harpoon, which he did. The fish promptly streaked off, hit the end of the rope and snapped the steel cable between the rope and harpoon head. Fortunately, the large circle hook held firm in its jaw and about two minutes later—now with the assistance of his handyman—Murray once more had the halibut wallowing on the surface right beside the dock. He reached down and rammed a rope under the fish's gill plate and out through its mouth, after which the two men grabbed the doubled rope and hauled the huge fish unceremoniously onto the deck. The dozen or so guests who had crowded closely around to watch and photograph the performance scattered like a covey of started quail as the 139-pounder suddenly started ricocheting noisily around the deck in their midst. From start to finish the entire process took about 6 minutes.

I can also recall productive trips off the west coast with Dick Close, former owner of Weigh West Marine Resort in Tofino, as well as several trips in the Sayward area with Doug Field of Buzz Bomb and Zzinger fame while he was developing and field-testing his popular Halibut Spinnow. Also recalled are two days spent at Blackfish Sound with "Mr. Lucky Jig," the late Mike Robert of Comox, as he did his magic with a handline and one of his popular lures.

Then there is the Codfather Charters gang at Port Hardy—owner Ken Jenkins and guides Bill Shire, Derrick Stevenson and Big Jim Henschke. All have enviable track records for putting their customers onto halibut even while others are going fishless, so just being in the same boat with any one of them has always been a learning experience.

Larry and Janice Stefanyk have fished over a much broader range than my wife, Vera, and I and a lot more often. Among their favourite guides here on Vancouver Island are Bill von Brendel in Ucluelet, Corey Hayes at Corey's Fishing Charters in Port Hardy, Jason Mohl of Jay's Clayoquot Ventures in Tofino, Adrian O'Connor of Reel Obsession Sport Fishing in Zeballos and Brian Lacroix of Brian Lacroix Sport Fishing in Sooke. They are a knowledgeable group of guys who enjoy repeat bookings year after year because they produce results for their clients. In the following chapters Larry will reveal some highlights from his trips with them.

If a few brand names crop up more often than others, this is simply because they are in popular use. Berkley, for example, offers a range of soft plastic saltwater baits that in many cases were first on the scene in their particular category. Delta Tackle Company is another that I mention frequently, primarily because so much of this British Columbia-based operation's extensive line is aimed specifically at halibut fishing.

I should also point out that many of the items in the close-up photographs of tackle that appear in this book have been in active use, in some cases for many years. This accounts for the scratches, scuff marks, dings, dents, and discolouration that appear on some of them. In order

Bob Jones and *Silver Fox* skipper Ian Andersen prepare to stow a halibut in the refrigerated fish box.

to show a broad range of equipment, I also asked friends to loan me items that are different from those Larry and I have on hand. One particular box of terminal tackle that a certain friend loaned to us contained dozens of corroded circle, Siwash and octopus hooks. This provided me with an opportunity to clean most of them up (the worst ones were discarded) and store them individually in small, re-sealable plastic bags. To save him embarrassment, I won't mention the name of this friend, but his initials are Ralph Shaw.

It's also worth mentioning that only two days after writing the above comment, while I was rooting through a dark corner of my basement, I discovered a small tackle box filled with drift jigs and leadhead jigs with soft plastic bodies. It had been hidden there for at least three years and most of the contents were corroded and discoloured beyond redemption. But please don't tell anyone, especially Ralph.

Finally, we are indebted to Calvin L. Blood, a biologist with the International Pacific Halibut Commission in Seattle, Washington, for his invaluable assistance in tracking down some of the information, illustrations and photographs used in this book.

PART ONE

BIOLOGY AND RANGE

*A*uthor's note: Much of the information provided in this chapter is based on the extensive and ongoing studies that have been conducted over the years by the International Pacific Halibut Commission.

Pacific halibut (*Hippoglossus stenolepis*) range from the Sea of Japan to Baja, California and north to the Bering Sea. They are most plentiful from Alaska to Oregon, with the British Columbia coast an area of primary abundance. Long considered one of this province's most important commercial fishes, halibut also play an increasingly important role in the recreational saltwater fishery.

A commercial halibut fishery began on the West Coast as early as the 1880s but by the start of the First World War it was already obvious that stocks were suffering from overfishing. In 1923 Canada and the United States, recognizing that halibut is one of the most valuable food species in the northern Pacific, signed a convention to regulate the fishery—the first treaty to be concluded anywhere for the conservation of a depleted deep-sea fishery. The International Fisheries Commission—later renamed the International Pacific Halibut Commission (IPHC)—that was established as a result of this convention was given a mandate to manage and research stocks within the convention waters of both nations. Today the commercial halibut fishery is allocated to vessels in Canada and to individuals in the US and managed on a 9 month season with total closure during January when the spawning season is at its peak. The Commission has imposed the same month-long closure on the recreational fishery. The current [2007] daily bag limit for recreational anglers on either side of the border is two halibut of any size.

Halibut are fairly long lived, with females surviving up to 40 years or more and males about 25 years maximum. However, they are a slow-maturing species. Females don't become sexually mature until they are 8 to 12 years of age, though they eventually attain lengths of up to 8 feet and may weigh as much as 660 pounds. Males mature at 7 or 8 years, seldom grow longer than 4 feet and peak at about 40 pounds.

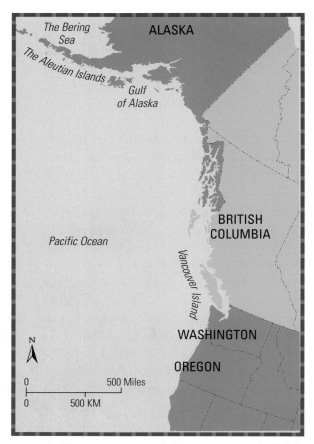

Halibut spawning occurs from December through February, which accounts for the coast-wide January fishing closure. Most spawning takes place in the Bering Sea, off the Aleutian Islands, and from the Gulf of Alaska southward to British Columbia, usually along the sloping edge of the continental shelf in water depths of 900 to 1,500 feet. Depending on a female's size, she may lay up to three million eggs annually. A 140-pounder, for example, may produce 2,700,000 eggs.

Fertilized eggs hatch in 12 to 15 days and begin drifting into the shallower waters of the continental shelf. At first it's difficult to tell a newly-hatched halibut from the larval form of other fish because it swims upright and has an eye on each side of its head. Its body is nearly colourless and quite transparent, which probably helps it avoid predators. The young fish initially feeds on the yolk sac from its egg and, when this is gone, feeds on plankton as the North Pacific currents carry it north and west. When the larval halibut is about an inch long, a strange transformation begins. The left eye migrates across the top of the fish's skull until it is positioned beside the eye on the right side. Its skull bones, nerves, and muscles all alter to suit this new form. Then, as the halibut starts swimming on its side, the right side begins to develop a mottled grey-brown colour while the left side becomes pale, almost white. When the young fish are about 6 to 7 months old, the prevailing currents carry them into shallower waters and they settle to the sea floor, perfectly camouflaged to become ocean-bottom predators.

They will spend the next five to seven years in this fairly shallow nursery area.

The growth rate of these juveniles varies, depending on location, habitat conditions and food availability. At first they consume small crustaceans and other benthic organisms but during their second year when they have reached about 12 inches in length, they become largely piscivorous.

Younger halibut, meaning those up to 10 years old, are highly migratory. Studies in the Gulf of Alaska indicate that they generally travel east and south in a clockwise direction, ranging throughout both shallow and deep waters during the course of a year. Although older fish are usually much less migratory, a few have been recorded travelling up to 3,200 km in order to reach their spawning grounds.

The body shape of an adult Pacific halibut is more elongated than most flatfishes, their width being about a third of their length. Their dark or upper sides may be light or dark mottled grey-brown depending on the colouration of the ocean bottom. The undersides are white, and some have reddish scratches and scuff marks. The consensus is that this damage occurs when the fish are migrating or perhaps when they are moving back and forth to feed in areas with gravel bottoms to those

The early growth stages of Pacific halibut. (Courtesy of International Pacific Halibut Commission)

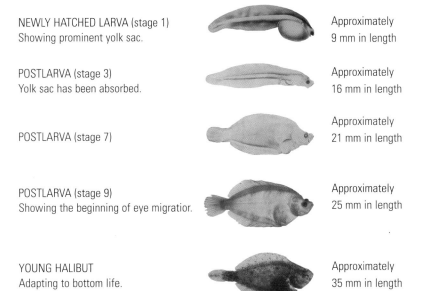

NEWLY HATCHED LARVA (stage 1)
Showing prominent yolk sac.

Approximately
9 mm in length

POSTLARVA (stage 3)
Yolk sac has been absorbed.

Approximately
16 mm in length

POSTLARVA (stage 7)

Approximately
21 mm in length

POSTLARVA (stage 9)
Showing the beginning of eye migration.

Approximately
25 mm in length

YOUNG HALIBUT
Adapting to bottom life.

Approximately
35 mm in length

Codfather Charters guide Bill Shire and friend
Choon Fong with a brace of typical "chickens."

with rocky bottoms. The only common predators for halibut in the North Pacific are sea lions, orcas and salmon sharks.

Both commercial and recreational fisheries refer to small halibut as "chickens" and large ones as "barn doors," but there is a sliding scale of what is small and what is large. Depending on where you happen to be fishing, a chicken might refer to a halibut weighing less than 10 pounds—or 20 or 30 or even 50 pounds. However, most anglers I have encountered seem to agree on 30 pounds. Likewise, a few start referring to fish of 60 pounds as barn doors, but the majority consider 100 pounds more realistic.

Halibut are found anywhere from very shallow waters to depths of at least 3,500 feet, but most are encountered at depths of 175 to 1,300 feet. (It should be pointed out that few recreational anglers fish much beyond 300 feet deep.) Being large, opportunistic feeders as adults, they eat a wide range of bottom fish, crabs, prawns, shrimp and squid, but they will also feed well up from the bottom, swimming right up through the water column to target schooling herring, pilchards and sand lance, and on occasion have been observed feeding just beneath the surface. During the salmon spawning season halibut will move in close to some river mouths to feed on the dead salmon that wash downstream into the estuaries.

The most common fish species you might encounter while halibut fishing are lingcod and members of the rockfish family, usually quillback, bocaccio, vermilion or the highly prized yelloweye. Lingcod, especially large ones, are active fighters that usually give both anglers and tackle a good workout. As lingcod longer than 36 inches are most assuredly females of prime breeding age and as they are not affected by swimming up and down through the water column, they can be safely released, hopefully with nothing worse than a small puncture wound in the jaw from your hook. Unfortunately, rockfish cannot adjust to the decompression, and they usually arrive at the surface with swim bladder distended through the mouth and eyeballs ruptured. As the daily possession limit on this species varies from one on the Island's east coast to three along much of the Island's west coast, halibut anglers should move away from areas where there appears to be an abundance of rockfish.

Arrowtooth flounders, incorrectly called turbot by some, are annoying critters. They are the same shape as halibut and grow to approximately 33 inches in length, which certainly puts them into the "chicken" class. However, don't get your hopes up, for their flesh is soft to the point of mushiness and their taste leaves much to be desired. While halibut are mottled grey-brown, the arrowtooth is dark brown; its mouthful of sharp, cone-shaped teeth is another giveaway. Let them go.

Commonly called "red snappers", this yelloweye rockfish was caught on a dink jig with a glow green hoochie.

Various species of skate (big, longnose and sandpaper) may also be confused with halibut but only until they are drawn close enough to the surface to reveal their diamond-shaped bodies and long tails. Both the flesh and liver are edible, but this fish must be cleaned, skinned and chilled very quickly. Some say that the flesh tastes similar to scallops while others compare it to crab.

Some species that you catch on an expedition for halibut won't even have fins. These include interesting things like starfish, octopus, sea anemones, nudibranches, and coral, most of them reeled up only after a desperate tug-of-war that threatens to break the line. While some can be rather repulsive-looking, slimy, shapeless white blobs, others have colourful, fragile-looking fronds that belie the struggle it took to break them loose from their anchors. The finest book I have ever encountered for identifying whatever it is that my friends or I have dredged up is *Marine Life of the Pacific Northwest* by Andy Lamb and Bernard P. Hanby (Harbour Publishing). I find that its "Quick Reference Guide" provides enough visual details that I can

Occasionally what an angler thinks is a chicken halibut on his line turns out to be a skate like this little one.

turn to a specific section for closer identification. Hardly scientific but it works for me.

Something that I never have trouble identifying is a rock, of which I have landed 4 over the years. In all cases it was akin to pumping and lifting what felt like 20 pounds of dead weight and in all cases the rock proved to be about fist-sized—maybe 3 pounds at the heaviest but probably closer to 2 pounds. At time of writing, Larry has tangled with only one rock. He tells me that it was about the size and shape of a tangerine and felt like a bucket of cement while he was fighting it. I'm starting to think that I should have had my largest one mounted.

2 TACKLE AND ACCESSORIES

*I*t's true that people who are after salmon occasionally catch some awesomely large halibut. After all, most saltwater anglers fishing off Vancouver Island are usually targeting salmon and only switch to bottom fishing as a diversion, often using the same tackle. While much of their catch consists of rockfish and lingcod, in areas inhabited by halibut it's usually just a matter of time before one is encountered. Most are "chickens" of 15 to 30 pounds, but some are larger—much larger. A season seldom passes without reports of halibut weighing over 100 pounds being landed on salmon gear, but many of the truly large fish break off. Had the anglers been fishing for halibut intentionally with the proper tackle, most of those big fish would have been boated.

Whether dedicated halibut hunters favour rods and reels or hand-lines, they are usually prepared to handle whatever latches onto their

Terry Gjernes of Nanaimo often tackles halibut with his Fenwick Matrix composite fibreglass/graphite mooching rod, which is still a workhorse after two decades of heavy use.

hooks, even fish of 200-plus pounds. And when they finally have a big one wallowing beside the boat, they also have the equipment necessary to subdue it, secure it, and bring it on board, or more increasingly to release it.

Some of the best halibut anglers on the West Coast are professional fishing guides, which is understandable considering that each season finds many of them spending 500 hours or more pursuing them. The better guides have repeat customers year after year because they produce results. They accomplish this because they know their waters intimately, have comfortable, seaworthy boats, use the best equipment available for the task—and keep everything in peak condition.

Thanks to modern technology, the size and weight of halibut tackle has decreased dramatically in recent years. Rods that used to resemble pool cues with large roller guides, heavy, winch-like metal reels and thick, stiff lines have been replaced by relatively lightweight rods and reels and strong lines of amazingly small diameter.

If you are new to halibut fishing and plan on purchasing your own tackle, please take your time and ask for advice. I have fished with people who own expensive, top-grade rod-and-reel combinations that were better suited for only heavyweight fish, not the chickens normally encountered in these waters. These anglers tired out quickly, and in most cases ended up borrowing tackle that weighed much less yet was still capable of handling fish of 300 pounds or more—if necessary.

If you use the services of a fishing guide or have friends who fish often for halibut, ask for their opinions about which brand names have good track records for dependability and pay attention to their advice and suggestions about what might best serve your purposes. Don't be afraid to direct your questions to a local tackle shop operator. You might suspect he will have a tendency to sell you only the most expensive equipment in stock, but this is seldom the case. Successful store owners get that way by having steady customers, which they get by treating them honestly.

Rods

Some rods designed for halibut fishing are constructed of fibreglass or a fibreglass/graphite composite. Others combine a graphite butt section with a fibreglass tip. Rods with 100 percent graphite shafts are available, but they are more expensive, and the truth is they do not stand up to being banged around in a boat as well as fibreglass or composites do.

Inexperienced anglers often abuse halibut gear unintentionally, and most rod breakages occur when an angler is pumping upward on the rod to lift a fish and raises the shaft straight up to the vertical position. This causes the tip to bend down too sharply and shatter. Ken Jenkins and his guides at Codfather Charters, which has a fleet of five boats fully equipped for salmon and bottom fishing, discovered that these breakages were occurring because on most rods the rear handle—the portion behind the reel seat—is too long. Codfathers greatly reduced breakages by shortening the rear handle by just two inches.

Preferred overall rod lengths range from 5 ½ to 7 feet. Some anglers favour roller guides throughout, but stainless steel ringed guides with ceramic inserts are much lighter in weight and do not abrade the line. Many rods incorporate both styles, some with a roller butt guide and roller tip guide, while others use only ringed guides and a tiptop.

Janice Stefanyk hooked this hefty lingcod while deep trolling a Tomic Plug off the west coast of Vancouver Island.

Ringed rod guides (top row) are lighter than roller guides (bottom) and require less maintenance.

A Shakespeare Tidewater rod is typical of the style and length preferred by dedicated halibut hunters and professional fishing guides.

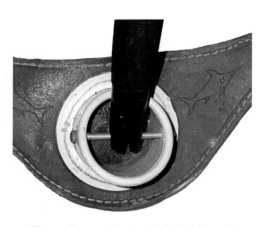

The steel cross pin in the fighting belt's cup fits into the rod handle's slotted gimbal to prevent twisting and serve as a fulcrum.

A typical Codfather Charters rod is a 5½-foot-long Shakespeare Tidewater model, of which about one-half is covered by the handle. Designed for "stand-up" fishing, the butt end of the handle has a gimbal that fits into a fighting belt, which is worn around the angler's waist. The horizontally-slotted gimbal fits over a steel cross pin in the fighting belt's cup; this prevents the rod from twisting sideways while reeling in, jigging or fighting a fish and creates a fulcrum for pumping and lifting upward under pressure. If your rod does not have a gimbal, it is a simple matter to remove the cross pin from the cup. The end cap on the rod handle will then fit into the cup and still provide a fulcrum.

Reels

Ideally, a reel should be a multiplier with a level wind, a fast retrieve, an easily adjustable and smooth drag, and a capacity of at least 200 yards of 50- to 80-pound test braided or thermal bonded line. A fast gear ratio is a boon when reeling in to check the condition of your lure or bait. Penn 114H reels are favoured by Codfather Charters for their durability and dependability, but Penn makes other models that incorporate more graphite in their construction, which makes them lighter in weight. Other manufacturers such as Ambassadeur, Shimano Shakespeare and Daiwa also offer a range of excellent reels.

Alvey makes a 9-inch diameter, single-action reel that some anglers use for halibut. I tried one and found that it retrieved about

A 9-inch diameter Alvey single-action reel.

2 feet of line for each revolution of the handle. Unfortunately, I caught no fish so can't comment on how it felt in use, but having used smaller single-action reels extensively, I see no reason why it wouldn't be fine. It would certainly add a new dimension to the give-and-take of line, and with so few moving parts there should be few if any maintenance problems.

Lines

The four basic line choices are nylon monofilament, braided Dacron, thermalbonded gel-spun polyeth-

Clockwise from the top: Walker, Penn and two Ambassadeur reels.

ylene (GSP) monofilament and braided GSP. Nylon monofilament is the most economical and has the best abrasion resistance, but it also has the largest diameter for its strength and a stretch factor of up to 30 percent. Braided Dacron of the same test is slightly smaller in diameter

Having the right fishing line is vital when reeling in a barn door halibut.

Western Filament TUF-Line was one of the earliest lines made from braided Spectra (gel-spun polyethylene).

than nylon monofilament and has only 10 percent stretch. Thermal-bonded GSP monofilaments fall between nylon and braided Dacron in diameter and cost, have no discernible stretch, and are a good choice.

Braided GSP lines, which are sold as Spectra and Dyneema, are the most expensive by far, but as they might last for several seasons, their initial cost is justifiable. I took the plunge in 1993 and plunked down $68 for 500 yards of 50-pound-test Izorline braided Brutally Strong Spectra. At time of writing I am still using it, which makes it 13 years old. I don't consider that a bad investment.

Like the thermal-bonded lines, braided GSP has less than 5 percent stretch and offers the smallest diameter-to-strength ratio. Depending on the brand, 50-pound-test is usually of similar diameter to 10- or 12-pound-test nylon monofilament. I proved this for myself when, after making my first purchase, I removed the 200 yards of premium grade, 30-pound-test nylon monofilament from my Ambassadeur 7000 reel and replaced it with the 50-pound-test Izorline—all 500 yards of it. I eventually hacked off 200 yards and gave it to a friend, so he could try it, and wound the remaining 300 yards onto an Ambassadeur 6500.

Small diameter is a major consideration while bottom fishing because tidal current pushing against a fishing line creates "surface ten-sion" between the rod tip and the terminal tackle. The larger a line's diameter, the more surface it has for a current to push against. The line will develop a belly throughout its central portion, which lifts the ter-minal tackle from the bottom—yes, even with a 2-pound sinker or jig on it. As the rod's tiptop guide acts just like a hinge, with 100 yards of line out it is quite possible for the terminal tackle to sweep upward until it is 50 feet or more above the bottom. As surface tension relates

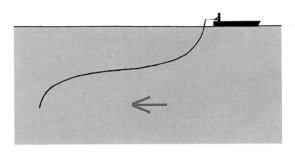

The tidal current pushing against a fishing line creates surface tension that can lift a 2-pound jig right off the bottom.

directly to a line's diameter, a braided GSP line of such small diameter might provide up to 30 minutes extra fishing time at each end of a slack tide than is possible with monofilament of equal strength.

However, while some anglers swear by braided GSP lines, others swear at them. In fact, I know of several who purchased braids when they first became popular in the early 1990s, used them only once or twice and then went back to nylon monofilament or Dacron. And they do have a negative side. Despite the hyperbole by manufacturers about their particular brand of braided GSP having good abrasion resistance, the ones I use—ranging from 30- to 100-pound-test—are notoriously poor in that respect. I discovered almost immediately never to use free-sliding lures like Buzz Bombs and Zzingers with them for they will scuff the material to the point where the line parts and the lure is lost. Why is anyone's guess, but it happens. If fishing with this style of lure, use a barrel swivel and a short nylon monofilament leader that tests somewhat weaker than the main line. I tie up several of these ahead of time and keep them separately stored in plastic bags. With a Duo Lock or McMahon snap on the end of my braided line, lure changes are accomplished quickly and easily.

Another negative aspect of braided GSP line is that it is so soft that it will often throw a loop around your rod tip while jigging. This can

Rigging a few drift-jigs ahead of time and sealing them in plastic bags allows you to change lures quickly and easily.

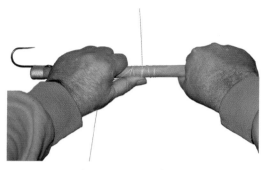

When pulling on braided gel-spun polyethylene line to free it from a snag, always
wrap it around a wooden dowel, fish club
or gaff handle. Never *ever* wrap it
around your hand or fingers!

have drastic results if you set
the hook on a fish—especially a
large one—and it starts to run,
which they always do.

Early users also found that braided GSP's lack of stretch resulted in
multitudes of broken rods when anglers reacted too vigorously to
snagged lines and large fish. A lot of these broken rods were constructed from fast-action graphite, which probably helps account for
the resurgence in popularity of fibreglass with its softer action and more
forgiving nature when abused.

Then there were the horror stories of anglers grabbing a snagged
line and taking a wrap or two around a hand in order to jerk a snagged
lure loose. This is something that you don't want to do at the best of
times, let alone from a fast-drifting boat. Unless you are wearing a
glove, don't even reach out to grab a line in order to pull a fish closer
to the boat for harpooning or gaffing. If a lure or bait snags on the bottom and can't be jiggled free, slack off the line and make several wraps
around the wooden handle of a gaff hook, fish club, or simply an 8- to
10-inch length of wooden dowel kept handy for just that purpose.
Make a half dozen wraps, then another half dozen back over top of the
first ones, then hold the handle,
club or dowel with both hands as
the slack is taken up and a strain
applied.

Knots

Because they are so soft and slip-
pery, GSP braids are notoriously
undependable at holding traditional knots. As a result, several
knots have been developed or
modified to rectify this situation,
and there is now a 42-page book-
let available that covers this topic

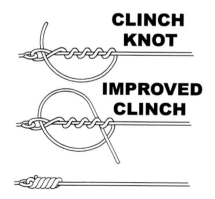

CLINCH KNOT

IMPROVED CLINCH

The clinch knot and improved clinch knot
are suitable for large diameter nylon
monofilament line.

A simple Palomar Knot is dependable for tying hooks, swivels and lures to braided gel-spun polyethylene line.

in detail: *Geoff Wilson's Guide to Rigging Braid, Dacron and Gelspun Lines*. It deals with a range of knots, loops and splices, and even devotes several pages to knot tests conducted on various brands of GSP lines. If your local tackle shop doesn't have one, try www.amazon.ca.

The general consensus is that one of the most dependable knots is a Double Palomar, which is formed by tying a regular Palomar with the line doubled. Nevertheless, I have managed quite well over the years by tying on swivels, hooks and lures with a regular Palomar Knot, so have no reason to change.

Filling a Reel Spool:

If braided line is not reeled in under tension, it has a maddening tendency to bury itself between other wraps of line on the spool—so deeply and tightly at times that it is necessary to cut the line. The best way to initially fill a reel with braided GSP is to mount the reel securely on the rod handle, thread the line through the butt guide and level wind guide, then tie it to the spool using a Uni Knot with at least 12 turns. Next place a magazine flat on a chair or table. Drop the line spool into a suitable container (a small box or can) so it can turn freely, and then lay the line across the centre of the magazine. Stack enough other magazines

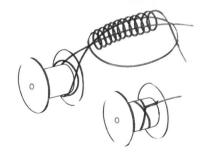

A Uni Knot is best for anchoring braided gel-spun polyethylene line to a reel spool.

on top of the line until the desired tension is achieved, and then fill the reel to the proper level—about 3 mm (⅛-inch) from the rim.

Braided gel-spun polyethylene line should be initially spooled onto a reel under steady tension.

Another thing to bear in mind about GSP braided lines is that virtually all manufacturers underrate them to compensate for the fact that most will lose an average of 25 percent of their strength at a knot. This underrating varies from manufacturer to manufacturer, but many 50-pound-test brands actually test at anywhere from 60- to 80-pound-test. This is something to remember if you happen to be trying for an International Game Fish Association halibut line test record.

Splicing Braided Fishing Line

1. Fray end of 80 lb. test, No. 2, thread through eye of darning needle.

2. Insert long darning needle in 120 lb. test.

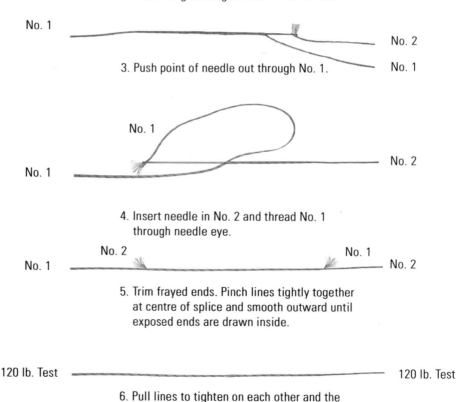

3. Push point of needle out through No. 1.

4. Insert needle in No. 2 and thread No. 1 through needle eye.

5. Trim frayed ends. Pinch lines tightly together at centre of splice and smooth outward until exposed ends are drawn inside.

6. Pull lines to tighten on each other and the splice is complete.

A needle splice creates a dependable, small-diameter joint between two braided lines. The line will usually break before the splice will fail.

Splicing Braided Lines

Codfather Charters has been using braided line for many years (Western Filament's TUF Spectra), and it's worth noting the way they load it onto their reels. Each spool is partially filled with 130-pound-test braided Dacron, to which is needle-spliced 200 yards of much smaller diameter 130-pound-test braided TUF, and then another 10 feet of 80-pound-test braided Dacron is needle-spliced onto the end. By joining the lines together in this manner, the full strength of each is realized. As most of their bottom fishing is done at 300 feet maximum (occasionally deeper), the 200 yards of main line is ample. Partially loading the spool with the cheaper Dacron helps fill it to capacity and speeds up the retrieval time when cranking in to check the bait. Large halibut can be handled on the 80-pound-test Dacron, while if a jig solidly snags bottom, the line will part at this weak link, thereby salvaging the more expensive GSP main line.

Despite the shortcomings of braided GSP lines, those of us who have learned a few simple rules for their use are quite happy with them and have no intention of backtracking: 1. initially wind line onto the reel under tension, 2. use a dependable knot, and 3. always keep an eye on your rod tip while jigging. I won't claim that you can feel a fish swimming past your braided GSP line, but you can certainly feel the slightest of movements when a fish mouths your bait or nudges your lure, and when you lift your rod to set the hook the reaction at the other end is instantaneous.

Handlining

This tactic, which is nearly as old as fishing itself, remains popular with a fair number of bottom fishermen for good reason—an experienced handliner can often hook halibut while the rod-and-reel set remains fishless. A typical outfit consists of a line holder fashioned from 5-ply marine grade plywood, 200 yards of 150- to 300-pound-test nylon

For storage, a handline is simply wound onto a wooden line holder.

This Lucky Jig Handline Reel is used only for storing the line, not fighting a fish.

monofilament, and a jig weighing from 1 to 2 pounds. Although some outfits incorporate a large reel fashioned from metal or high impact plastic on which to store the line, a reel of this kind is not used for fighting fish. This is always done by hand.

The larger a line's diameter, the easier it is to handle and coil on a boat deck without tangling. The main drawback is its susceptibility to "surface tension"—water pressure pushing against the line, which causes it to belly upward and stream in the current even with a 2-pound jig on the end. **The late** Mike Robert used a 150-pound-test handline with his 1-pound jigs, claiming that he could actually feel the lure down to 400 feet in calm water. For his 1 ½-pound jigs he used 200-pound-test, which he said worked equally as well to the same depth. Robert said 300-pound-test loses its sensitivity at about 300 feet, so he didn't use it at all.

Ian Anderson recommends that a new handline be thoroughly stretched before use. He ties an old hook and sinker on the end, lowers it into fairly shallow water and then intentionally snags bottom. Backing the boat off, he lets out the full length of line and stretches it for about five minutes. He claims that the stretched line will lie in loose coils when pulled in, making it much easier to handle.

Mike and Ian were in agreement that, when tying a knot in line of such large diameter, it is necessary to ensure that it is seated properly. Mike used an improved clinch knot with five turns then sprayed it with WD-40 before tightening it. Ian uses a Trilene knot but first heats the end over the oil stove in his boat's cabin until it becomes soft and pliable.

Ian also advocates wearing light rubber gloves when handlining. "Leather gloves get wet and quickly become a smelly mess and cotton gloves dry like rocks. I use rubber gloves—the kind you buy for washing dishes—but they're only half the thickness of cannery workers gloves so they eventually cut and tear and you have to trash them."

Tackle Containers

"Terminal tackle" covers all of those expensive items that go on the business end of your line: hooks, sinkers, swivels, snaps, split rings, leaders, spreader bars, and lures. In cases where only bait is used, the tackle collection might consist of nothing more than a few single hooks, swivels and sinkers, but most halibut hunters have fairly substantial collections of drift jigs, leadhead

Tackle boxes can be large or small, and simple or elaborate in design.

jigs and top-rigged pipe and dink jigs, often intermingled with dozens of soft plastic action lures and baits plus large, colourful hoochies. So it stands to reason that when dealing with so many heavyweight items, the container chosen to store and transport them should be sturdily constructed. There is, however, another important point to consider when selecting a container: overall size and carrying capacity. After a quarter century of experience, I eventually discovered a system that actually works: I now use large tackle boxes for storage and travel purposes, and smaller ones for ready-use once at my destination.

There are four basic container choices, all of which come in varying sizes: standard tackle boxes with internal storage trays, soft-sided modular systems with several storage containers, heavy-duty canvas bags, and storage boxes of wood or plastic. Each has good and not-so-good points, but no matter which style of container you choose, view it as a rust and corrosion factory for anything made of metal. I have three truly huge, multi-tray tackle boxes, none of which are used for saltwater tackle of any kind, let alone halibut gear. All are of sizes that, if filled to even half capacity, they would create a hernia-inducing load best carried in a wheelbarrow.

Standard tackle boxes may have a hinged or double-cantilevered top or a hinged front that opens to reveal drawers. The problem with most is that you must fit various items into compartments that are often too large or too small for the purpose, though some have adjustable compartments that can be configured with sliding baffles that lock into place, providing some degree of control. Better yet are those designed for bulk storage, but only if they are of a manageable size overall. My favourite is a fairly large (8 x 10 x 16 inches) Rubbermaid model, which unfortunately is no longer in production. If you happen to find one in a store or on e-bay, grab it.

Single-side and double-side plastic briefcase-style tackle boxes are my favourite choice for terminal tackle, jigs and soft plastic lures because they hold a reasonable amount of items and are easy to keep clean. Most have adjustable compartment baffles, which means that even a few pipe jigs or large soft bodies can be stored.

Another of my ready-use containers is an ancient Old Pal tackle box measuring 5½ x 6 x 13 inches, which is fashioned from some sort of heavy-duty black plastic. It was purchased in the late 1960s, and when the metal hinges failed about 10 years later, I replaced them with an 11-inch length of piano hinge held in place by 14 small nuts and bolts. I didn't bother replacing the trays, and the amount of tackle it holds is impressive. Yet another is an el cheapo kid's red plastic tackle box that probably sold for a couple of bucks. It's fashioned from one piece of moulded plastic. I get a kick out of taking it along just to see the look on peoples' faces, but at 4 x 5 x 12 inches with no internal trays, it easily holds enough tackle to get me through a day of fishing. I use it mainly for bulky, lightweight items like hoochies and soft plastic action lures, plus a few leadhead jigs.

Soft-sided tackle systems are certainly a consideration, for their tray-style boxes have slotted compartments with baffles. These work quite well with the storage, travel, ready-use system I prefer because a single one of these boxes will usually hold enough lures or terminal tackle for a

Using a soft-sided tackle system makes good sense as you need remove only one utility box for taking on the water.

day's use. Okay, maybe two boxes——which is when a smaller heavy-duty canvas shoulder bag comes in handy.

Plastic storage containers are available in a wide range of sizes, and while some anglers prefer large sizes–Ralph Shaw's favourite is 5 x 11 x 16 inches—I lean toward the smaller ones, especially if fishing with bait is on the agenda. These hold hooks, swivels, snaps and whatnot, and even the bait itself, all of which fits into my canvas shoulder bag. And there is usually enough room to fire in a couple or three leadheads or dink jigs—just in case.

This basic terminal tackle selection will remain in peak condition if the components are stored in self-sealing plastic bags.

The problem with hooks, swivels, snaps and metal lures is they are susceptible to corrosion. All you have to do is take them out on a boat and the salt air will start having a detrimental effect. Splash a drop or two of saltwater into the container or toss a wet hoochie into the mix, and nasty, metal-eating grunge is guaranteed. Can it be avoided? Of course. All you have to do is invest in a supply of self-sealing plastic bags, which are available in various sizes from plastics supply stores and some hardware stores. Get plenty of the little 2 x 3-inch size to store your large single hooks individually. Placing treble hooks in plastic bags can pose a problem, but punctures can usually be avoided by sliding a short length of flexible small-diameter plastic tubing over each

point. Cocktail straws work on a fair range of mid-sized hooks, and for large hooks, try milkshake straws. For storing larger items like hoochies and soft plastic bodies, use the plastic bags meant for food. Overkill? Not when you are paying a dollar or more for some hooks.

After sharpening treble hooks, force a length of plastic straw or tubing over each point before storing them separately in plastic bags.

I am now an admitted self-sealing plastic bagoholic who keeps items contained in them until time for use and replaces wet items in them after use. I keep these used items separate until I can rinse them off with fresh water, oil them if necessary, and place them in new plastic bags. Admittedly it takes some fussing around, but the money saved has done wonders for my bank account. If you have hooks that are already corroded, soak them in a strong solution of trisodium phosphate (TSP), rub them down with fine steel wool, lightly oil them, and store them in their own bags. They might still be discoloured, but they won't rust any further and can still be used.

While I was compiling the material for this book, my friend Ralph Shaw dropped off three plastic storage containers of halibut tackle for me to photograph. In one of them I found a dozen no. 10/0 Siwash hooks that he'd had brazed in order to close the gaps in the eyes, figuring that if the hook twisted within the knot there was a possibility (albeit remote) that the line could be cut. This brazing had annealed the eye and part of the shank of each, and now all of them were terribly corroded. A few minutes with TSP, steel wool and 3-In-One Oil soon had them all serviceable again.

Terminal Tackle

At its simplest, bottom fishing with bait means suspending a leader and hook below a heavy sinker, baiting it, and then tossing it over the side. If the sinker is fixed, this is called a mooching setup; if the sinker slides freely on the mainline it's known as a fishfinder setup. Variations to both types are dependent on the sinker style and shape. Another variation is to tie a 3-way swivel between the main line and a leader to which a sinker is tied on the end. A shorter leader and a hook are then tied to the swivel's side loop.

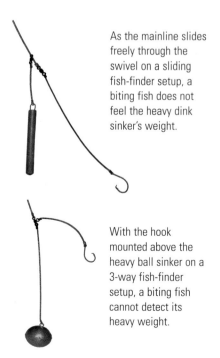

As the mainline slides freely through the swivel on a sliding fish-finder setup, a biting fish does not feel the heavy dink sinker's weight.

With the hook mounted above the heavy ball sinker on a 3-way fish-finder setup, a biting fish cannot detect its heavy weight.

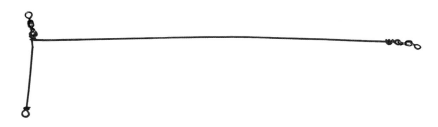

Although available at most tackle shops, a spreader bar can also be easily fashioned from heavy stainless steel wire or from a coat hanger.

All of these setups work fine in shallow water, but at the greater depths where halibut are found, as everything plunges toward bottom, the leader and baited hook tend to stream back and wrap around the sinker and main line. This is resolved by using an L-shaped spreader bar constructed from stiff wire. Although available commercially, spreader bars can also be fashioned from coat hangers, but because of saltwater corrosion they won't last long, so stainless steel of similar diameter is a better choice.

To make an L-shaped spreader bar:

Using round-jawed pliers, bend a right angle into a length of wire so that one arm is 20 inches long and the other 4 inches long. Next bend a loop at the right angle and loops at the end of each arm. Just before closing the loops at the right angle and at the end of the long arm, install a large barrel swivel in each of them. In the loop on the shorter arm install a Duo Lock snap or simply use a length of nylon monofilament of a lighter test than the main line to tie on a heavy sinker. The leader that you tie between this spreader bar and your hook should be no longer than 12 inches— shorter is even better. Using a leader longer than the spreader bar's longest arm defeats its purpose, often with even worse tangles.

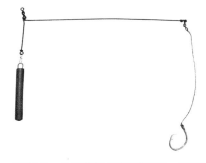

The dink sinker is attached to this spreader bar with a Duo Lock wire snap. Note that the leader is slightly shorter than the spreader bar's long arm.

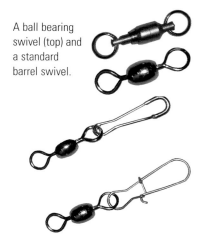

A ball bearing swivel (top) and a standard barrel swivel.

Both the McMahon (top) and Duo Lock snaps are fashioned from a single length of wire. The McMahon is stronger but the Duo Lock, being smaller in diameter, is a better choice for jigs and lures that depend on movement and action to attract fish.

Sinkers

Most tackle shops have an absolutely confusing range of sinker shapes and weights on display, but for halibut fishing we can reduce the preferred styles to three basic shapes: ball, cylinder (dink) and keel. Ball-shaped and dink sinkers generally range up to 24 ounces; keel sinkers, which are more commonly used for trolling and mooching for salmon, range up to 16 ounces. For deepwater halibut fishing with standard tackle, always opt for the heaviest weights available. Light tackle enthusiasts must experiment to determine which weights work best for them.

Swivels and Snaps

Whether you choose ball-bearing swivels or standard barrel swivels, never place them all in the same container. Plastic bags are a lot cheaper than swivels. (Being rather frugal by nature, I prefer barrel swivels.)

The only wire snaps to consider are the one-piece McMahon— which must be the strongest available on the market—or the one-piece Duo Lock. I lean toward the latter, finding them easier to open and close. Also, when inserted into the eye of a leadhead jig or trolled plug, a Duo Lock's smaller diameter wire does not hinder their movement or action.

The three basic sinker shapes are cylindrical, ball and keel. Keel sinkers can be fixed (middle photo) or semi-fixed/sliding (bottom).

Single Hooks

Stiff competition between hook manufacturers has resulted in anglers having a wide choice of high-quality, specialized hooks from which to choose, yet their prices have remained fairly reasonable. While stainless steel hooks are still the most resistant to corrosion, there have been great inroads made with non-stainless steel hooks, most of which are fashioned from high carbon steel (HCS) or from alloys using HCS as a base, such as VMC's vanadium steel. As HCS is subject to rapid corrosion in salt-water, these hooks are either lacquered with a protective coat-

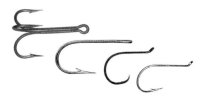

(Top to bottom) Basic hook styles include treble, Siwash, circle and J-hook. (J-hooks have the most shape variations.)

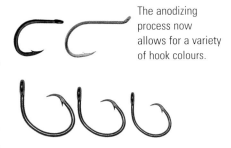

The anodizing process now allows for a variety of hook colours.

Although designed for fishing with bait, circle hooks are often used with spoons, top-rigged jigs, and even flies.

ing or plated through an electrolytic bath process called anodizing. At one time bronze, japanned (black), gold, silver, nickel and tin were the standard finishes and colours available, but anodizing has seen the introduction of long-lasting finishes in red, blue, green, grey and black.

Although traditional hooks are J-shaped, most manufacturers now offer circle hooks, which feature an extremely short shank with an almost circular bend that continues right on through the point. Their hooking and holding qualities make them the choice of commercial longline fishermen, and many anglers targeting bottom fish with fresh bait also prefer them. The general consensus is that while more fish are lost on the bite, those that are hooked stay hooked. The most important thing to remember when using a circle hook is when you feel a bite, DO NOT SET THE HOOK! Fight the urge and wait. You are better off, in fact, to give the fish a bit of slack line. After ingesting the bait, the fish will turn and start swimming away. As the line tightens, the fish, feeling the line's pull, may try to disgorge the bait, or the line's tension might cause it to pull freely out toward the jaws. WAIT! Then, when you feel a steady pull, start reeling in to further tighten the line. In

Tying 2-hook tandem setups ahead of time and storing them in self-sealing plastic bags saves time when out on the water.

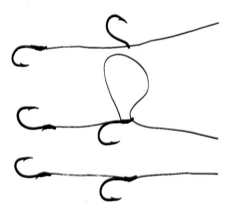

Tying a 2-hook tandem setup.

virtually all cases the fish will be hooked in the hinge of its jaw, which makes unhooking it much easier.

There was a period when pundits maintained that circle hooks should be used only while fishing bait, but this is no longer the case. Flies are now tied on circles, salmon anglers use them on metal spoons for trolling, and some halibut buffs use them on their top-rigged pipe or dink jigs. While it is virtually impossible to thwart bait-stealers, they can be slowed down if your hook sizes match the bait and your intended quarry. Although no. 6/0 singles are popular for general use, anglers envisioning barn door halibut frequently opt for 10/0. Some feel that two hooks in tandem are more efficient than a single hook, and others anglers use three.

NOTE: Circle hooks and tandem rigs for use with top-rigged jigs are covered in that section.

To tie a tandem rig:

Use single hooks with a standard length shank and turned-up eye. Tie on the rear hook with a snell or shank knot and trim off the short tag end. Next thread the leader's free end through the eye of the second hook from back to front. Slide the hook down the leader to the desired position, then bend the leader back sharply

behind the hook eye and make 7 to 10 tight wraps rearward around the shank and the piece of leader leading back toward the rear hook. While holding the wraps tightly between thumb and forefinger, thread the leader's free end back through the hook eye from back to front and then pull it tight. That's all there is to it.

Treble Hooks

Although most Norwegian jigs, top-rigged jigs and drift jigs come from the manufacturer with treble hooks, fishing guides and experienced halibut anglers usually replace them with one or two large single hooks. While the design of a treble might place one of its three points in position to hook into a fish's jaw, it simply does not hold as efficiently as a single hook, which has a larger gap between the point and shank and therefore a better bite.

Because of the wide gap between the point and shank of a single hook, its holding ability is superior to that of a treble hook.

It's a different story with bottom-rigged drift jigs such as Pirkens, Buzz Bombs and Zzingers. Because of their flattened, fish-shaped bodies, while being jigged up and down, they have a tendency to turn sideways on the drop then flutter or rotate horizontally until the line tightens. As a result, with these jigs you will likely hook more fish with a treble than with a single. Of course, you will also lose more because they are not as well hooked, but this is the price of compromise.

Flowing 5-minute epoxy into the rear section of the treble hooks used with drift-jigs and spoons will prevent the line from jamming between the shanks.

Another problem with drift jigs occurs because of the way they are manipulated in the water: they will occasionally flip over in such a way that the line catches

behind the hook bend and then pulls up tightly and jams between the rear ends of the shanks. When this happens you will be jigging away, blissfully unaware that your lure and hook are hanging upside down and totally useless. To eliminate this problem, the closed gap treble hooks from Buzz Bomb-Zzinger are brazed farther to the rear. When you are using standard treble hooks, you can avoid snagging your line in this way by mixing up a small batch of 5-minute epoxy and flowing it between the shanks right back to where the bend starts curving up on each hook. (Note: This trick accounts for the brown blobs that appear

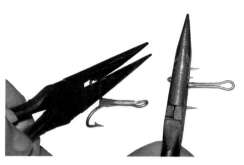

A barb should be crushed at the widest point of the pliers jaws by squeezing straight down, never at an angle.

in the pictures of treble hooks in this book.)

The *BC Tidal Waters Sport Fishing Guide* states that if you are fishing for salmon or trout in tidal waters and using treble hooks, the barbs must be pinched flat or removed. While barbs are permitted for halibut and other bottom species, many of the drift jigs that are suitable in size for them are also attractive to salmon, chinooks in particular. This being the case, crushing the barbs flat makes good sense. Do so by gripping the hook point and barb from the side close to the rear of your pliers' jaws and squeezing slowly until the barb flattens against the shaft.

Sharpening Hooks

Dull hooks probably account for most of the missed strikes and lost fish that we experience or hear about. Never assume that, just because you seldom snag bottom, your hooks won't become dull. The bony mouth of a fish does an excellent job of blunting sharpened points, and rust and corrosion also take their toll. And although most anglers associate dull hooks with excessive use, the sad truth is that many new hooks right out of the package are in need of sharpening.

When sharpening a hook, you must consider the style of the point:

Spear: Most commonly found on mass-produced hooks of low cost, the spear possesses fairly good penetration qualities. It is the easiest point to sharpen.

Needle: With its tapered, cone-shaped point, the needle has excellent penetration qualities but tends to dull easily. Siwash hooks usually have this point style.

Hook point styles (left to right): spear, needle, hollow and circle.

Hollow: Common on top quality salmon hooks, the hollow point has good penetrating and gripping qualities.

Circle: This point is usually needle-shaped and bent inward as much as 90 percent about halfway between the barb and the tip. Once set, a hook with this point style seldom pulls free or falls out.

Both the spear and needle point should be sharpened with a fine-cut flat file and then honed with a flat-surfaced stone. Hollow and circle points should be serviced initially with either a fine-cut round or rat-tail file then finished with a cylindrical stone. An automotive point file is another tool that comes in handy for touching up points.

Small Tools

A well-equipped boat will be stocked with an assortment of tools and small items that are used anywhere from occasionally to frequently. Heading the list are needle-nose pliers with sidecutters; these are used for cutting fishing line, pulling knots tight and removing and rebending hooks. Pliers of this kind are used so often that many anglers carry an extra pair in a pocket or on a belt holster. Stainless steel "floating pliers" with buoyant handles are expensive but worth the money when they are dropped accidentally over the side.

Split ring pliers are another handy though often overlooked tool that save a lot of frustration and broken fingernails. Most manufacturers also make needle-nose pliers that incorporate a split-ring snout or tooth, but these are a compromise, and I find that the tooth gets in the way when I have to remove a hook from inside a fish's mouth. Although they generally have three indentations in the jaws that may be used for crimping metal sleeves, I prefer a separate set that is specifically made for opening split rings.

Other items that should be in your boat when you head out for halibut include a club or hammer with which to stun the fish, a sharp

XTools floating pliers and needle nose pliers with side cutters serve many purposes, from cutting line to crushing barbs to removing hooks.

general duty knife for bleeding them and for other general cutting jobs, a filleting knife, a filleting glove, a large carborundum stone or ceramic sharpening rods for keeping knives sharp, a small carborundum or India stone for touching up hook points, a board for cutting bait, a container of light oil or WD-40, a file for sharpening hooks and gaff hooks (spray it lightly with WD40 and keep it in a plastic bag) and a selection of "wipers" (small terry cloth towels are ideal).

Split ring pliers prevent broken fingernails and frayed tempers.

"Multitools" such as those manufactured by Leatherman, Gerber, and Swiss Army are popular with many anglers, though more especially with fishing guides who must make adjustments and small repairs to various tackle items during the course of a day's work. But some of the tools in these collections border on the ridiculous, so a good rule of thumb is to select one that has only the tools that will most likely be required.

Note that I have recommended that you carry two knives in your boat because a filleting knife should be sharpened at a shallow angle of

To sharpen a hook point:

Always stroke the file or stone from the barb toward the tip of the point at an angle of approximately 20 degrees toward the upper plane of the point. The general idea is to remove metal only from the sides and top of the point until the desired taper has been attained. Once satisfied with the shape of the point, use a stone to hone the tip to a needle-sharp point. The bottom of the point should receive a minimum of honing as it tends to alter the line of entry if too much metal is removed. To sharpen a needle point, simply follow its natural contour from the barb to the point, but be very careful to remove metal evenly all the way around it.

The simplest method of testing a hook for sharpness is to lightly drag the point across your thumbnail. A properly sharpened hook will etch the surface of the nail and try to dig in, while a poorly sharpened point will simply glide over the surface without catching.

To sharpen a hook point, always stroke the file or stone from rear to front.

about 10 degrees, which actually weakens the cutting edge and makes it unsuitable for hacking at anything harder than skin or flesh. The edge of a general purpose knife blade should be sharpened at the more acute angle of about 20 degrees, which is plenty sharp enough for most cutting jobs but allows the knife to withstand the abuse of cutting through the spine of a large fish.

Filleting Knives

Filleting knives tend to be similar in shape and design, with the two most popular blade styles being scimitar—slightly curved and tapering to a slender point—and needle—fairly straight and uniform in depth throughout its length but curving upward into the point. This latter blade is similar to the boning knives used by butchers and meat cutters. I have owned and used both styles for many years and can't say that one design has any advantage over the other. My own knives include Gerber, Buck and Schrade Walden, but the one that always seems to be in my tackle bag is a Rapala with a 6-inch blade. I find that it handles most filleting jobs quite well but must admit that on fish over 50 pounds a 9- or 10-inch blade works better.

With knives you definitely get what you pay for. High-quality steel is seldom if ever found in cheap knives. They may appear every bit the equal of knives costing three or four times as much, but generally the blade will prove to have the edge-holding qualities of virgin lead. Each of the materials used for the handles of filleting knives has its selling points. Wooden handles may be easily shaped with a file and sandpaper to customize the fit in your hand; synthetics are virtually indestructible and easy to keep clean; cork handles float the knife in case of an accidental dunking; and the gritty finish usually found on metal handles offers a superior grip for slime-covered hands. Spend some time hefting various knives and you should be able to come to a conclusion

Filleting knives may have straight or slightly curved blades.

about which feels most comfortable in your hand.

Keep the blade of your filleting knife razor sharp. A dull knife is a dangerous implement. A keen cutting edge slices easily through skin and flesh with little pressure; a dull one requires more force combined with a sawing motion—and this is what often leads to accidents. Never abuse your filleting knife by cutting through bones or other hard material, and when the knife is not in use, protect the blade by putting it in its sheath.

A sharp knife is a pleasure to use: a dull knife is an accident waiting to happen.

Sharpening Stones

Among the popular sharpening stones available on the market are carborundum, India and Arkansas. Some are equipped with a fine-grit surface on one side and coarse-grit on the opposite, while others, such as those made from natural stone like Arkansas, come in one grit only. If it comes down to a choice between coarse and fine, opt for the latter. Choose a rectangular stone with a minimum length of six inches. If you can get a longer model, do so. The initial cost may seem high if it is a quality stone, but it will pay for itself in sharpening efficiency and long life.

Harpoons

A large landing net with a sturdy frame and strong mesh will handle halibut of up to 50 pounds, but anything larger is usually harpooned or gaffed. The most popular harpoon has a bullet-shaped, toggle-style head that pulls free of

Corey Hayes aimed his harpoon head just behind the gill collar of this 98-pounder then let it fight the buoy for a while before landing it.

To get that sharp edge:

Use both hands for the task.
The hand gripping the handle maintains the angle of 10 degrees from horizontal. The fingers of the other hand are spread out along the back of the blade to either push or draw the blade across the stone's surface while supplying the pressure necessary to ensure an even bevel to the cutting edge. The pressure should be just enough that the gritty surface can be felt biting into the metal. Undue pressure will result in an uneven cutting edge and a swaybacked sharpening stone.

Use both hands for the sharpening task.

1. Place the base of the blade on the stone with the handle at a right angle to the stone.
2. As you push the blade forward along the stone, start pulling the handle slightly rearward.
3. As the cutting edge nears the point, continue pulling the handle rearward and lift it slightly to maintain the proper angle. Use the entire length of the stone.
4. For the opposite side, the cutting edge is placed on the stone so that it faces you. Draw the blade toward you, pivoting and raising the handle as necessary to maintain the proper angle.

5. Repeat these steps until the cutting edge is razor sharp. Once properly sharpened a good piece of steel should need only two or three strokes with a fine-grit stone on each side of the blade after each use to maintain its razor edge.

If the blade is extremely dull or badly nicked, it may be necessary to attack it with a file. Wrap the handle in several layers of thick cloth and grip it carefully in a bench vise, or simply grip the handle tightly and rest the rear of the blade against something stable as you file. A machine grinder should never be used since the cutting edge might lose its temper from overheating.

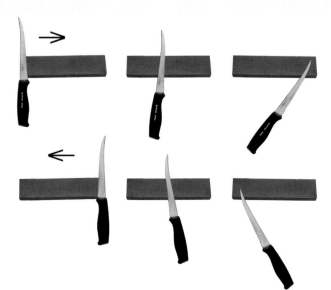

Throughout the sharpening sequence, try to maintain the same angle along the edge.

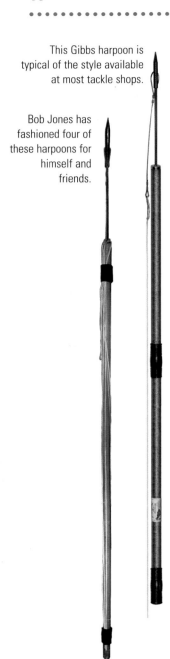

This Gibbs harpoon is typical of the style available at most tackle shops.

Bob Jones has fashioned four of these harpoons for himself and friends.

the shaft after it is thrust through a fish's body and then turns sideways to prevent it being pulled out again through the hole. It pays to keep the hole in the rear of the harpoon head and the shaft-end that fits into it clean and very lightly lubricated. If you fail to do this, you might plunge the harpoon head through a large halibut, only to have it pull right back out through the hole because it has jammed on the shaft. I have seen this happen on occasion, and it makes for some very interesting and exciting antics on the part of the fish and everyone involved.

There are three options with the harpoon rope: hang onto it, tie it to a boat cleat or tie it to a buoy that can be thrown over the side. All have their advocates. Hanging onto the rope is fine with small fish, but anything over 100 pounds might create problems unless you are wearing gloves—and have enough rope in case it happens to be a 250-pounder intent on swimming back down to the bottom. Tying to a boat cleat also has its drawbacks, especially on some of the smaller boats where cleats have been known to rip loose from the gunwale when a large halibut made its run. And even if the cleat does hold, the rope might break. If you decide to use a buoy, its size may depend on how much storage room is available in the boat. The idea is to create drag against which a harpooned fish must constantly fight, but it must be buoyant enough to float it to the surface. Something about 16 inches in diameter is usually sufficient. Allow about 20 feet of rope from the harpoon head to the buoy's attachment ring.

In the late 1980s I made the first of four harpoons and gave it to Ian

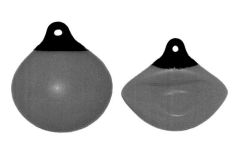

This type of buoy, available in various diameters, can be deflated for easy storage.

Using a large buoy reduces the effort and danger after a large halibut has been harpooned.

Andersen. Unlike commercial models, its brass head was fastened directly to 30 feet of nylon parachute cord. Over the years he used it to land some very respectable halibut, one weighing 220 pounds. When this harpoon was about 10 years old, Ian used it on a large halibut that promptly took off, but as soon as the parachute cord was fully stretched, it snapped off about a foot from the cleat to which it was fastened. When a harpoon rope breaks, the head's weight usually pulls the rope through the wound, so even if the fish is landed, the harpoon head is lost. However, at precisely the moment the parachute cord broke, the Lucky Jig's treble hook pulled from the fish's jaw. The fish would have been lost at this point, but by a quirk of fate one of the jig's hook points slipped into a small loop that had been accidentally knotted in the parachute cord, and Ian found himself back in business. He eventually landed the fish by using a flying gaff. It weighed a very respectable 200 pounds.

In 1991, while fishing near Stubbs Island in Blackfish Sound, Mike Robert landed a 254.7-pound halibut while handlining with a Lucky Jig—quite an accomplishment while fishing solo from a 16-foot welded aluminum boat. However, later that year he wasn't quite as lucky. He hooked a much larger halibut that he guesstimated to be at least 300 pounds. "I was using 550-pound-test nylon parachute cord for a harpoon rope," he related. "When I harpooned it, that fish took off and hit the end of the rope, snapped it like a piece of string and kept right on going. My hook pulled out at the same time, so it was goodbye, Mr. Halibut. Now I use a 30-foot line with a bungee-cord on the end so it doesn't snap when they hit the end."

Corey Hayes uses a gaff hook to haul a hefty halibut into his boat.

Gaff Hooks

A "striker gaff" has a straight, 5-inch spike angling at 30 degrees from its sturdy wooden handle. It's meant to swing downward into a fish's head with a hard, hammer-like blow. After hauling a fish over the gunwale, this "hook" is removed, the handle reversed and used to club the catch. However, as the stiletto-shaped hook comes out as easily as it enters, it's a poor choice for suspending a thrashing fish over the side of a boat. And since a striker gaff is best used while standing, it is unsuitable for use in a small boat.

To fashion a handle for a flying gaff:

1. Cut a 12-inch length from the unflared end of a piece of ¹¹⁄₁₆-inch outer diameter PVC electrical conduit that is flared out at one end to form a ferruled joint. Position one end against the hook shank opposite the point. Mark the conduit in line with the inside rear of the hook eye. Use a half round file to form a shallow, 1.5-inch oblong slot in the handle to accommodate the rope. Use a sharp knife to widen inside the slot.
2. Use masking tape to position the conduit against the shank so the slot and hook eye are aligned.
3. Use heavy nylon thread to bind the shank tightly to the conduit. Start by wrapping the thread back on itself for one inch then make tight, even wraps toward the eye. Remove the tape.
4. One inch from the end lay a loop of 50-

Attaching a handle to a shark hook makes it easier to set in a halibut and to remove.

pound-test nylon monofilament against the handle. Continue wrapping over it to the eye, then use the loop to pull the tag end back under the wraps. Coat the thread with clear Varathane. After it dries, wrap over the thread with ⅛-inch diameter braided polyester drapery cord. NOTE: Fray both ends for one inch so they lie flat. Finish with two coats of Varathane.
5. Splice the braided rope to the hook eye then thread it through the hole and out the handle's top end.

A "gaff hook" is shaped like a large barbless fishhook. It is pulled upward or sideways to impale the fish through the lower jaw or shoulder area. Because of the gaff hook's shape, you can use it to suspend your fish over the side while you stun it with a club or hammer before lifting it into the boat.

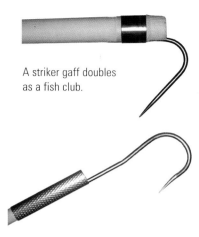

A striker gaff doubles as a fish club.

A typical gaff hook.

The so-called "flying gaff" is simply a large, barbed shark hook (no. 16/0 to 20/0) with a length of ⅜-inch braided polypropylene rope or nylon parachute cord spliced to its eye. If your boat has low gunwales, you can hold the hook by its shank while reaching down to set it in the fish's jaw or head. However, attaching a short handle makes this task just that much easier as well as safer when treble hooks are involved. After setting a flying gaff, you can control even a large fish with the rope.

A large shark hook can be used as a flying gaff.

A "handling gaff" is used to lift smaller fish up off the deck and place them in the fish box and its handle is useful for wrapping line around when snagged on the bottom. You can make one from ¾-inch diameter wooden dowel and a no. 10/0 Siwash hook with the barb crushed flat. Simply drill the dowel to accommodate a ½-inch wood screw that fits through the hook eye then bind the hook shank to the handle with heavy nylon thread and coat it with clear Varathane.

Tethers

Tethers are 10- to 15-foot long coils of ⅜-inch braided polypropylene rope or nylon parachute cord, each looped at one end to fit over a boat cleat, and stiffened at the other end so it will slide easily under a fish's gill cover and out through its mouth. Lay about 18 inches of stiff

A handling gaff is used for moving fish and also comes in handy for pulling on a snagged fishing line.

stainless steel or coat hanger wire against the unlooped end and wrap it tightly with two layers of plastic or duct tape. A halibut can be hung over the side by a tether and bled by cutting across the bottom of its gill arches. This quickly weakens and kills the fish, enhances the colour and quality of its flesh, and increases its frozen storage life.

To stiffen the end of a tether, use plastic or duct tape to bind a length of stainless steel or coat hanger wire to it.

3 BAIT AND LURES

*I*t's frustrating to feel a fish chew on your bait for a while and then stop, leaving you to wonder if anything is left down there on the hook. Of course, the only way to find out is by reeling in to check its condition. While this can be annoying if you are fishing in 50 feet of water, it becomes downright tiring and painful if your bait is down around 500 feet. (Yes, some people actually fish that deep!) The process of cranking in, re-baiting if necessary, then dropping back down takes several minutes. When added up over a typical day, a lot of productive fishing time is missed, and muscles that you didn't even know existed in your arms and shoulders will probably be protesting mightily. Thus, knowing all you can about baits and lures will mean less wasted time and energy.

Fresh and Frozen Bait

When choosing fresh bait to dredge along the bottom for deep-water species like halibut, lingcod and yelloweye rockfish, you should consider the findings of the US National Marine Fisheries Service, which conducted extensive research on the Alaskan commercial longline halibut fishery during the late 1970s and early 1980s. By working from inside submersible vessels, the scientists were able to closely observe

Fresh or frozen herring are attractive halibut bait but they are easily torn from the hook.

what actually happened to the baited hooks suspended from the longlines.

The aroma of fresh herring quickly attracted various fish species and other creatures like snails, starfish and crabs. Being soft, however, the herring disappeared so rapidly that the scientists found it difficult to estimate the loss rate. Pieces of octopus and Pacific grey cod stayed on the longest, which was attributed to neither one of them attracting

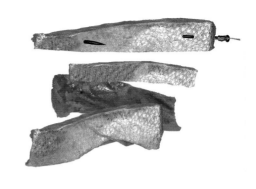

Strips of salmon belly are as attractive as herring and much more durable.

much interest rather than to their durability. The best all-round bait by far was salmon. Its scent quickly attracted interest and its durability meant that it stayed on the hook longer. Remember this the next time you fillet or clean a salmon. Save all scraps with the skin intact—especially the white-skinned belly meat—and save the heads and skeletal remains of smaller salmon such as pinks and sockeye. Salmon or other fish that has become freezer-burnt due to extended or improper storage is another source of bait. Although unpalatable as table fare, halibut will find it quite edible.

Freshly killed fish also work as bait, especially rockfish and greenling. Some might question recommending the use of rockfish when they are totally protected in some areas and restricted to one fish per day in others. There is, however, nothing written in the *BC Tidal Waters Sport Fishing Guide* that states a legally caught rockfish must be recycled through the intestinal tract of a human being, so whether it is eaten or used as bait is strictly up to you. The best compromise, of course, is to save the fillets for consumption and use the remains for bait.

The Berkley Power Mullet has a paddle-shaped tail that produces a side-to-side swimming action.

Filleting a small fish yields three baits—two fillets with the skin left on, and the skeletal remains. If the fillet is fairly large, cut it lengthwise into narrower strips. Fillets are best rigged with two single hooks in tandem, one through the thick neck portion, the other through the thinner tail section. Insert the front hook through the skin from the flesh side, then reverse it and push the point back through the skin so it protrudes from the flesh side. The tail hook need only go through the skin once. If using a filleted carcass, insert the front hook through the skin behind the head and the trailing hook wherever it fits best. While fishing in Blackfish Sound in 1993, Lynn Gerig of Lebanon, Ore., used the remains of a filleted rockfish to attract a 259-pound halibut.

Pretty well anything edible works for bait—anchovies, needlefish (sandlance), pilchards (sardines), shiner seaperch, butter and horse clam necks, squid, shrimp, prawns and crabs. Even

Lynn Gerig landed this 259-pounder in Blackfish Sound in 1993. His bait was the filleted carcass of a rockfish.

"unnatural baits" work on occasion and there are many accounts of halibut biting on fresh beef, pork and chicken flesh, garlic sausage, and Smoky wieners.

Fresh or frozen squid can be used whole or in pieces, but being fairly soft it rates no better than herring for longevity on a hook. But while it's impossible to prevent squid from being torn loose by bait-stealers, the process can be slowed to a manageable level by using two hooks in tandem, and then crisscrossing the hooked bait with tight wraps of heavy thread or dental floss (I prefer waxed). Cut about three feet of thread and half-hitch one end around the leader ahead of the front hook's eye, leaving a tag end four inches long to serve as the anchor point. As squid swim backwards, insert the front hook through the tail and the trailing hook through the head. After positioning the hooks, wrap the thread rearward, covering the body and binding it tightly to the hooks and line, then forward again to the tag end of thread. Tie the two ends together and you are in business.

Bait Bags

While preparing small bags of salmon roe for winter steelhead fishing, Bill Shire got the idea of covering herring chunks with the same strong, red mesh. He later discovered that, while the mesh will eventually tear, it lasts long enough to make herring a viable bait for use with spreader bars or jigs. Yet another tactic is to stuff a bait bag inside a hoochie. If the filled bag's diameter is slightly larger than the inside diameter of the hoochie, the flexible plastic of the hoochie will stretch enough to hold the bait firmly in place where it can produce a scent trail.

Bait bags can also be filled with other fish scraps, chopped squid, clams or mussels, or crushed shrimp or prawn heads with the sharp spines broken off. Place a golf-ball-sized mound of bait in the centre of a 4-inch square of mesh, fold the edges of the material up over the top then bind it tightly with strong thread or dental floss. (Unlike the attention to detail required for preparing and rigging cut-plugs or herring strips for chinook and coho salmon, neatness doesn't count much where bottom fish are concerned.) For even more durable bags use pieces of nylon panty hose or what I consider to be the ultimate—the plastic mesh from a vegetable produce bag. Any of these bait bags can be frozen prior to use. Radiant Lures makes a hollow plastic bait holder called the Gun Barrel that fits inside the large hoochie used with their Halibut Hammer pipe jigs, but these ultraviolet holders may be purchased separately for use with other jigs. As the Gun Barrel is semi-rigid, its contents last even longer than if it were in a mesh bag.

Various baits can be used in mesh bags, but herring is especially good because of its aroma.

Just remember that while bait often outfishes lures, it also attracts increased interest from dogfish. Whenever these pesky little sharks prove to be a nuisance, consider switching to a leadhead jig, top-rigged jig or a drift jig without bait.

Scent

The date when humans first began using scents to attract fish is unrecorded, but it probably goes back to the practice of "chum-

The Gun Barrel from Radiant Lures is used for attaching fresh bait or scent to halibut lures.

ming"—that is, introducing chopped-up bait into the water to attract fish. Whatever the origins, various preparations have been around for years, among them the "natural" oils of anise, vanilla and garlic. I stress the word "natural" because these days many scents are derived from blends of chemicals.

When well-known author and television personality Charlie White was producing his series of outstanding underwater films about salmon fishing, he discovered that if scented and unscented lures were trolled side-by-side, salmon almost always hit the scented one. Never mind that the foul-smelling, oily water from his boat's bilge seemed to be the most attractive scent of all, the point was that once a salmon started following two lures trolled side-by-side, scent definitely made a difference in creating follow-through takes. When Charlie discussed his findings with scientists at the University of Washington School of Fisheries, he was told that his bilge water probably contained some of the same amino acids and aromatic hydrocarbons that they were experimenting with at the time to learn the effects of scents on fish. Charlie started working with these scientists, and the result was his popular Formula X-10 scent. He doesn't have a lot of film about how halibut react to scented and unscented lures because they are difficult to locate with underwater cameras, but what he does have is a lot of positive feedback from happy customers who swear by his Formula X-10, many of them professional fishing guides.

So where does scent fit into the overall picture? Where salmon are concerned, sight is probably first on the list. A salmon sees a flasher, which draws it closer, whereupon it spots the lure or bait trailing behind the large attractor. As it closes in on this possible food source, it probably starts picking up sonic waves through its lateral line, confirming that what it sees might be something good to eat. But then again, maybe not. That's why fish don't bite every time.

While those studies by the US National Marine Fisheries Service revealed that herring scent attracted almost instantaneous interest from virtually all fish, and grey cod and octopus were of the least interest, what octopus did have going for it was durability. Thus, octopus worked best when combined with a more aromatic bait like herring. One provided scent, the other something to chew on, hopefully long enough to get the fish hooked. While many halibut anglers continue to use this sort of a "bait kebob," more are discovering that using octopus with a liberal dose of scent works just as well. Most of these saltwater scents are based on herring, anchovy, sardines, squid and shrimp, and they are available in liquid form, pastes, gels, mouldable dough and sprays. Determining what to buy is simply a matter of asking someone at your local tackle shop which one sells best. If a specific brand of scent is a best seller, it's usually for a very good reason: anglers might fall for over-hyped products once but they won't keep buying something unless it works.

Can you make your own scents? Of course. A friend creates a real witch's brew that doesn't endear him to his wife but does attract halibut and other fish. He simply drops a load of shrimp heads into a blender and zaps it until it turns into a thick paste. The pureed shrimp is then tied up in squares of nylon stocking as detailed in the Bait Bags section and stored in the freezer. The bags can be impaled on a hook, stuffed up inside of a hoochie, or inserted in a Radiant Gun Barrel. This is about as simple as it gets and it will probably work in a similar fashion with various small fish like herring and sardines or with salmon scraps.

A fairly recent offering from Berkley is a strip of Saltwater Gulp Cut Bait that, according to the company, disperses 400 times more scent than any other bait or scent. I hesitated at paying over $12 (taxes included) for a strip 2 ¼ x 7 ½ inches long, white on one side and chartreuse on the other. Theoretically, however, if only a tiny piece is required to add powerful, long-lasting scent to a lure, that modest-sized strip should last for several trips. It has a natural skin texture and is available in 10 colour combinations.

There was a time when many anglers praised WD-40 spray lubricant as an effective scent, and I'm sure that some still use it as such. The company, however, does not promote this in any way, and as more people become concerned about water quality, the practice of using it is in question.

While fishing scents attract with positive smells, they also mask negative smells. Back in the 1960s, *Outdoor Life* magazine published an article that stated handwashing before touching fishing lures or baits would increase your luck. Fish, it claimed, have a negative reaction to the smells produced by human hands, one culprit being L-Serine, a tasteless, odourless chemical found in the natural oil of our skin. Other negative smells include stuff we handle, such as gasoline, sunscreen lotion and insect repellent. I tried washing beforehand and it worked.

Action Baits

A few years ago Berkley increased the length of their curly-tailed Power Grub to 8 inches. The new model is biodegradable, loaded with scent, available in a range of colours, and includes a large, crescent-shaped tail that wiggles enticingly when drawn through the water. Fishing guides and halibut hunters were quick to try them on their spreader bars and with heavy leadhead jigs, and just as quick to discover that the "right" colour could be a winner. The emphasis here is on "right" because it changes from place to place, day to day, and even from hour to hour. The general consensus is that glow white is the best all-round choice but at times other colours attract the action. As a result, it pays to

David Wei took this chicken on a Delta Tackle Chub Grub while fishing out of Port Renfrew.

Berkley Power Grubs were first on the halibut scene, but other manufacturers were quick to follow with their own models.

Foot-long Chub Grubs from Delta Tackle offer halibut a real mouthful.

have a selection of colours on hand. Other manufacturers now offer similar soft plastic action baits, providing an even wider choice from which to choose. If you believe that size counts, consider Delta Bait's Chub Grubs, which are scented, curly-tailed action baits available in lengths of 10 and 12 inches. But if one curly tail creates action, are more even better? Possibly. And this accounts for the popularity of lures like Delta Tackle's Double Fin and Jumbo Tails. They also make Curly Skirts, colourful, multi-fringed collars that fit between a leadhead jig head and the soft plastic body or hoochie, creating even more colour and action.

Yet another family of soft plastic action baits are the shad minnows. The paddle-shaped tail wags back and forth as the minnow is drawn through the water, providing a lifelike swimming motion, but the tail's motion is also said to have a sonic effect. To date the largest I am aware of is 6 inches long, but it's probably only a matter of time before a manufacturer offers them in larger sizes. Latest on the shelves as this is

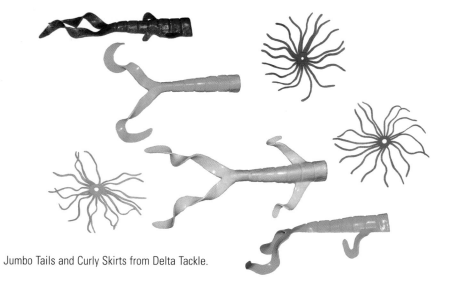

Jumbo Tails and Curly Skirts from Delta Tackle.

being written in early 2007 is Berkley's Power Mullet line, which looks mighty promising.

When not in use, store all soft plastic baits in self-sealing plastic bags to keep them clean and maintain their scent.

Lures

There are four basic types of lures used for halibut: heavyweights of 1½ to 2 pounds, middleweights of about 12 to 16 ounces, drift jigs weighing 6 to 10 ounces, and trolling lures like plugs and spoons. Depending on weather and water conditions, all can be fished at the depths necessary to locate halibut. Drift jigs often prove attractive to salmon and other species and can be fished with much lighter tackle.

Norwegian Jigs

Oldest by far of the heavyweight, metal-bodied lures used for bottom fishing is the Norwegian jig, also called a cod jig. Used by commercial and recreational fishermen throughout the world, it is shaped like an elongated, trian-gular teardrop

Norwegian jigs can also be top-rigged.

with the heavy end at the bottom. This is also where the large treble hook is located, which can prove a real problem when fishing around rocks and sea anemones. Some anglers switch the hook to the top end and add a hoochie to it to reduce the hang-ups.

Pipe Jigs

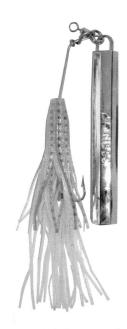

Gibbs Mudrakers are typical of the "pipe jig" family.

As the name implies, a pipe jig is usually a length of metal pipe filled with lead and then rigged at the top end with a large hoochie. The most popular kinds used in Vancouver Island waters are the Lucky Jig, Gibbs Mudraker, Delta Giant Skirt and Radiant's Halibut Hammer, which range in weight from 1 to 1½ pounds. All are equipped with treble hooks, but many anglers and guides exchange these for a large single hook or two singles rigged in tandem on 200- or 300-pound-test nylon monofilament. The hooks are then crimped into position using metal sleeves.

Dink Jigs

Many anglers and guides simply purchase cylinder-shaped lead "dink sinkers," which are about ¾ x 6 inches and weigh just over a pound, and use them

A sample of colours available from Pacific Bait & Tackle.

unpainted. Codfather Charters uses these almost exclusively, rigging them with either a single hook or two in tandem and fastening them to the wire loop along with a colourful hoochie. Although unpainted dink jigs have a great track record at catching halibut and bottom fish, painted dink sinkers in various colours are available from Pacific Bait and Tackle, and they make fine-looking top-rigged jigs.

Top-rigged dink jigs are quite popular but need not be painted in order to produce positive results.

Your hoochie assortment should have a wide range of colours.

According to Codfather Charters, their three most productive hoochie colours are black/orange, purple/red, and one combining black, bright green, yellow and red. Mike Robert rigged his Lucky Jigs with dark-coloured hoochies—red and dark brown with a lime insert—for the east coast of Vancouver Island but mainly light colours like lime, white and pink for fishing off the West Coast.

Leadhead Jigs

A leadhead jig is simply a blob of lead moulded onto a single hook that has the front part of its shank bent so both the attachment eye and hook point ride upward when suspended from a line. Leadheads may be round or banana shaped, both being fairly snag resistant; compressed laterally to sink faster and stay down better; or compressed horizontally to plane up or down depending on the placement of the eye. Placing it

The range of head weights, body shapes and colours is limited only by the imagination.

near the nose makes it better for trolling or casting and retrieving while placing it at the rear makes the jig head act just like a diving plane.

As the leadheads that are best suited for deep-water halibut fishing are designed to swim horizontally, the attachment eye should be positioned somewhere around the centre of the head so the jig tilts up when lifted, then down again on the drop. Although a jig can be tied directly onto the line, it will work even better if it is attached with a wire snap, which also allows it to be changed much faster than by cutting the line and retying.

Body dressings can be fashioned from feathers, hair, synthetics, slender rubber strands, or colourful, soft plastic bodies moulded into a wide range of shapes and sizes. Various scents can be added to produce smells attractive to fish, and some manufacturers offer soft bodies that are made from scented, edible plastics. Some of these soft plastic bodies are formed into shapes that produce a built-in action—crescent-shaped tails or fins give the appearance of swimming sinuously when drawn through the water while paddle-shaped tails wag from side to side, creating a low sonic hum.

Although leadheads don't get down to the bottom as quickly as top-rigged jigs, if there isn't too much current they can be quite effective when bounced slowly along the bottom. Just remember that as the line of pull is directly up into a fish's bony, upper jaw, you must make sure that the hook point is always needle sharp.

Use epoxy paint on jig heads to prevent damage when they come into contact with soft plastic action baits.

Some leadheads are painted, some are not, but they all catch fish. Delta

Tackle offers unpainted, bullet-shaped leadheads in weights of 12, 16 and 24 ounces, which is a good range for all conditions. But if you decide to paint your leadheads, don't keep them in the same box as your plastic lures because the chemical used to make plastic lures soft and keep them that way has the same effect on most paints, and this can make a real mess in your tackle box. You can also use a 2-part epoxy paint on your leadheads that will not react to the chemical in the plastic lures.

Drift jigs like this Zzinger are attractive to both halibut and salmon, but watch out for those barbed hooks.

Drift Jigs

Drift jigs are usually fish-shaped and somewhat lighter in weight than top-rigged jigs and leadheads—usually 6 to 10 ounces for halibut. They are favoured by "light tackle" enthusiasts and, while quite productive, must be fished under ideal conditions in order to get down and stay down there. These lures have the added bonus of being attractive to large chinooks and coho salmon, which often strike them while they are sinking. (I have noticed that ardent halibut hunters never seem to complain about these incidental catches.)

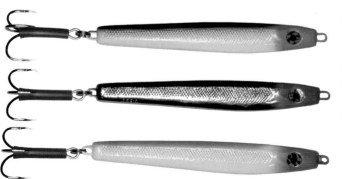

Gibbs Floorwalkers are available in weights of 6 and 8 ounces, making them suitable for light tackle halibut fishing.

Drift jigs come and go but those that produce good catches develop dedicated fans who do much to guarantee their longevity. Four old-time drift jigs that come to mind are Stingsilda, Pirken, Deadly Dick and the venerable Buzz Bomb. Newer kids on the block that come in sizes large enough to attract halibut hunters include Halibut Spinnow, Zzinger, and Gibbs Floorwalker.

Just as Rex Field introduced the slow-lift-rapid-drop jigging technique with his Buzz Bombs, Doug Field has his own advice for using a Halibut Spinnow: "Let it sink until you feel bottom, then lift it a foot or so. Instead of jigging it up and down, hold your rod tip low to the water and let the lure do its job. The body will hang straight down and rotate in the current, providing visual and sonic effects, and the pulsating action of the hoochie streaming out at a right angle to the body adds to the visual attraction. Concentrate on feeling for the bottom by lifting or lowering the lure so you can detect any changes in depth."

Whichever type of drift jig you decide to use, try sweetening the hook with a small piece of fresh bait or a healthy dollop of scent as this creates the added attraction of smell.

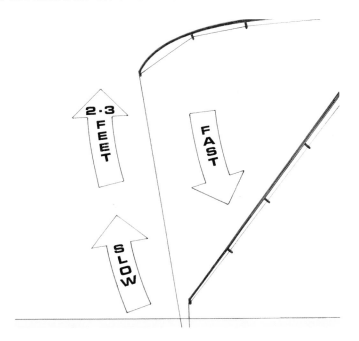

The slow-lift-rapid-drop jigging method developed by Rex Field for Buzz Bombs works quite well with all drift jigs.

Plugs, Spoons and Spinners

While plugs, spoons and spinners can all be fished with a heavy sinker, they work best when used with a downrigger. Spoons and spinners need be trailed only four or five feet behind the cannonball, but a plug should be far enough behind that its action is not impeded.

Standard salmon plugs like those from Tomic, Lyman and Luhr Jensen are most typically used, but don't overlook large, 7-inch-long Original Rapalas (F18) and FlatFish (T60). Rapalas have an enticing swimming action while FlatFish have a noticeable

A sample of spoon shapes and colours.

wobbling action at even the slowest of speeds. FlatFish can also be combined with fresh bait. Simply remove the front hook and tie at least three feet of thread to the tail hook hanger. Lay a small herring or strip of salmon belly along the lure's bottom, and then bind it in position by winding the thread forward and back before tying it off.

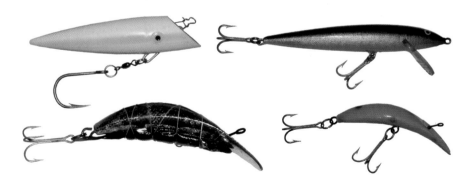

Typical plug shapes. Note that the FlatFish (lower left) has been rigged with bait.

4 DO-IT-YOURSELF PROJECTS

*T*here are three types of anglers found in all facets of fishing: those who purchase all of the lures and flies they use; those who make their own lures and tie their own flies; and the largest group of all, those who do a bit of both. Then there are the "modifiers"—those who purchase lures and make alterations to them, usually by combining lures or adding other components.

Top-Rigged Jigs

One of the slickest modifications I have encountered was a fairly simple yet innovative add-on to a top-rigged jig that was made by the ever-inventive Bill Shire, who guides full time for Codfather Charters. Bill is an active winter steelhead fisherman, and during his rambles along various North Island rivers he often finds bits and pieces of terminal tackle. Over the years he accumulated a fair number of "dink floats" fashioned from ¾-inch and 1-inch diameter cylinders of flexible foam plastic, and he decided they would fit quite nicely inside the large hoochies used with Codfather's top-rigged dink jigs.

So while making some tandem hook setups using 200-pound-test monofilament and aluminum sleeves, he cut a 2-inch length from the end of a dink float and punched a hole lengthwise through its centre. After mounting the rear hook on the leader and crimping it in place, he slid the foam cylinder onto the leader

Bill Shire's floating hoochie modification.

57

before mounting the front hook then pushed this modified tandem setup up inside a hoochie.When he suspended his modified jig in the water, the hoochie floated at a 90 degree angle to the body. Bill assumed that the foam plastic would compress as the jig went deeper but hoped enough buoyancy would remain to keep the hoochie horizontal—and the hooks in perfect position for setting into a fish's jaw. Indications are that he was correct in his assumptions. Customers using his prototype jigs immediately started hooking more halibut than those using unmodified lures. Among them was Stan Franczak of Red Deer, Alberta, who wrestled a 225-pounder to the side of Bill Shire's boat in June 1998.

As time passed, Bill continued modifying his invention, and the hook assembly of a typical Codfather Charters jig now has only one single hook. He points out six benefits to this change:

1.   It reduces the cost by one hook.
2.   It speeds up assembly time.
3.   The hook assembly's weight is reduced so it floats better.
4.   It cuts down on hang-ups.
5.   Less bait is required.
6.   There is one less hook to avoid while landing and handling a halibut.

Note: if you are lacking a dink float, any flexible plastic foam will work when cut to shape. I prefer white for its added visibility.

Another add-on that has its roots in steelhead fishing is the large Spin-N-Glo, which can be threaded onto the leader ahead of the hoochie before making the front loop. As these lures are buoyant, they also help hold the hoochie and hook up in position. Port Hardy guide Corey Hayes of Corey's Fishing Charters uses a large Spin-N-Glo ahead of a baited circle hook on his spreader bar setups. Corey is also a commercial diver so has actually been down on the bottom to observe first-hand how lures work—and how fish react to them. According to those who have tried this setup, it attracts bites much faster than unadorned bait on a spreader bar.

Leadhead Jig "Buzzbaits"

Leadhead jigs can be easily modified by the addition of an overhead Spin-N-Glo or spinner blade, also called a safety-pin spinner. This modification requires the use of sturdy stainless steel wire, round-nosed pliers, and wire cutters. Although the top loop at the bend might look like an attachment point, it is merely a guide through which the main line or leader is threaded. I make mine with a safety-pin attachment that clips onto the hook eye. As the wire shaft is of fairly small diameter, there is also room in the hook eye to attach a Duo Lock Snap.

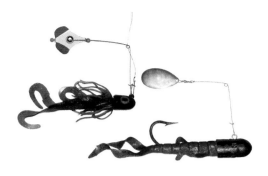

"Buzzbaits."

The best blade shape is a modified propeller that spins at the least bit of forward motion and creates a soft buzzing sound that attracts the attention of fish. These can be fashioned from sheet stainless steel, aluminum or brass, and may be painted or covered with adhesive Mylar tape. The main problem I have found with this style of lure is that if there are lingcod in the area, they simply won't leave it alone. While using these buzzbaits, I once cranked a 45-pounder up on one side of the *Silver Fox* while Vera was doing the same on the opposite side with a 60-pounder. As both were released, these weights are, of course, guesstimates.

To make a ball jig:

A length of stiff stainless steel wire can be used to fashion a simple, yet productive top-rigged jig that uses a ball-shaped sinker for its weight. Bend the wire as shown in the illustration and crimp the sleeves. The wire's length can be longer or shorter than shown, and the sinker weight can also be adjusted to suit your preference. The wire shaft can be left bare or covered with coloured plastic tubing like the child's skipping rope used for those shown in the illustration.

Push the long bottom end through the sinker and bend the end back in a U-shape about ¼-inch long. Use a hammer to tap the short end of the U into the lead. You may add a spinner blade or Spin-N-Glo to the shaft for added attraction and sound, but be sure to install a plastic bead to aid in its rotation.

The wire shaft on a ball jig can be as long or short as desired.

New Glow Ball sinkers from Pacific Bait & Tackle.

Drift Jigs

Drift jigs with a wire line attachment loop can be modified by
using a split ring to attach an in-
line spinner or Spin-N-Glo that is
mounted on a wire shaft. While a

A Spin-N-Glo in front of a drift jig adds a bit of
colour and motion.

Spin-N-Glo also works well with Buzz Bombs and Zzingers, in order to
prevent the buoyant lure from floating up the line, install a rubber stop-
per or a nail knot on the line in front of it. It will spin more freely if a
small plastic bead is mounted on the line behind it.

Moulding Lead Pipe Jig Bodies

Some of us mould our own jig bodies using molten lead. I must
warn you, however, that unless strict safety measures are followed,
this process can be downright hazardous to your health in three
ways: burns, blindness, and lead poisoning. Fortunately, the safety
measures involved consist mostly of following the common sense rules
of dressing properly, wearing eye protection, and working in a well-ven-
tilated area.

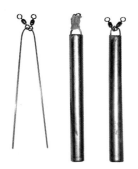

Taping the swivels at
the top of the wire
leaves ample room for
pouring the molten
lead into the pipe.

Making a Pipe Jig

As a pipe jig is simply a length of metal pipe of suitable diameter that has been filled with lead, you can
make your own by cutting a piece of pipe—brass,
copper, galvanized or plated steel—and blocking off
one end with masking tape. Next cut a 6 inch length
of $\frac{1}{16}$-inch diameter stainless steel or brass wire and
bend it into a U-shape about $\frac{1}{2}$-inch wide across the
centre. You may then slide one or two large swivels
onto the wire, depending on whether you intend to
attach the jig to your line with a wire snap. (When
rigged, the hook should always be attached to a
swivel.) Reverse the U and hold the swivel(s) in the
upright position at the top of the U while you secure them with masking tape. Alternatively, you can forgo the swivels and attach a large split
ring to the wire loop after the jig is formed.

Slide the two wire legs of the U into the pipe until the loop is about
$\frac{1}{2}$-inch above the pipe. Place the pipe upright in an empty coffee

Working with Molten Lead:

The basic requirements for moulding lead sinkers and jigs.

The best place to set up for lead melting and pouring is on a sturdy table or bench in a dry, well ventilated area—one where you need not worry about other people, children, or animals being anywhere near. If you must work inside, use an electric fan to suck fumes away from the melting pot and exhaust them through an open window or door, and take the added precaution of wearing a reliable respirator. Lead fumes are not only noxious, they accumulate in the body's organ tissues. Avoid breathing them at all costs.

Always dress appropriately for heating and pouring lead: wear shoes, long-legged pants, a long-sleeved shirt, and either goggles or a face mask. It takes less time to don protective clothing than to heal from burns, and it's much easier getting used to wearing eye protection for a while than it is to using a white cane or a seeing-eye dog forever.

On the table should be a heat source, a melting pot, a large spoon for skimming dross (impurities that float to the top of the molten lead), a container for the dross, either tongue-and-groove or Vise-Grip pliers, side cutters, two thick pot holders with which to grip the handle of the melting pot, and two 1-kg coffee cans (or something similar), one of which is filled with dry sand. Using cans of this size allows me to cast up to four pipe jigs or dink sinkers without crowding them, although you might actually squeeze in a half dozen.

I use a single-burner propane stove as a heat source and a discarded 6 inch cast iron frying pan as the melting pot. It is large enough to handle a 5 pound lead ingot, yet small enough that it can be used to pour the molten lead without transferring it to a smaller container. The frying pan has a handle that can be easily gripped with pot holders, a pouring lip that directs the flow of molten lead, and the rear side of the pan can be easily gripped with pliers.

Moisture and molten lead are an explosive combination. Never quench molten lead with water and never pour lead into a mould that has been cooled in water. If the splattering lead doesn't get you, your involuntary jerk reflex may cause the entire contents of the melting pot to spill and splash. Place the lead—either an ingot or pieces of scrap—in the melting pot. (I speed up the initial process by using a propane torch to add extra heat to the lead.)

After you have finished pouring, systematically shut down the melting operation and allow the equipment to cool prior to storing it away. (I store mine in our carport, which accounts for the rust on my frying pan.)

1-kg coffee cans serve as moulds.

The dross is skimmed off before the lead is poured.

can, leaning it against the rim. After inserting two or three more pipes, pour a few inches of sand into the can and stand the pipes upright so they are evenly spaced. Continue adding sand until it is an inch or so from the tops of the pipes.

You are now ready to pour the molten lead into each pipe, doing so in one slow, continuous motion. When each has been filled, go back to the first and top up if necessary. Don't worry about overfilling, for any lead that dribbles onto the sand can be replaced in the melting pot and reused. The sand will get quite hot, so allow it to cool before removing the jig bodies.

Making a Dink Sinker or Jig

An alternative to filling a metal pipe with lead is to use heavy wrapping paper as a "lost mould." You will require an 8- to 12-inch length of ¾-inch diameter wooden dowel, a supply of paper cut into 6 x 6-inch squares, and masking tape. You will also need a wire loop that is bent as illustrated to prevent it from pulling free from the sides of the finished body.

Wrap a square of paper tightly around the dowel and tape it shut along the outer edge. Slide the tube to one end of the dowel and place

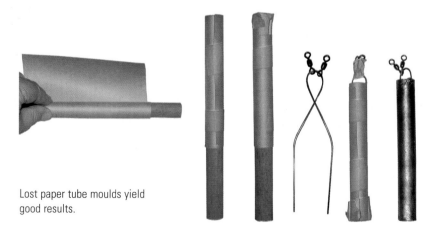

Lost paper tube moulds yield good results.

a couple of pieces of tape across the end. Remove the dowel and insert the wire. The remaining steps are the same as for making a pipe jig, but you will need to use enough sand to surround the tubes right to their top edges.

After pouring and cooling, the charred paper can be removed quite easily by simply peeling it away. If some is persistent, scrape it off with a utility knife or use a wire brush. The bodies can be used as is or painted if desired. Epoxy paint produces the longest-lasting surface and is impervious to the effects of soft plastic baits.

Each of the jig bodies shown on page 62 weighs about 18 ounces. To increase or decrease the weight, you can alter the length or diameter of the pipe or use a wooden dowel of smaller or larger diameter on which to wrap the paper tubes.

Making a Harpoon

During the mid-1980s I fell heir to various lengths and diameters of brass rods. They gathered dust in a dark corner of my cluttered basement, but after a halibut trip out of Port Hardy with Ian Andersen, I decided to try making him a toggle-head harpoon. It was the first of four.

I have a fairly decent workshop for doing the basic metal work required for this project: a large bench vise, a drill press, a large collection of files, and a hacksaw with an adjustable frame of tubular steel, which makes it rigid and comfortable to hold and use. A 12-inch blade offers the longest forward cutting motion, and 18 teeth per inch provide the fastest cutting for brass. (This teeth-per-inch information is marked on the blades.) Make sure that the blade is tight in the frame, as a loose blade will buckle or bind and wander off course. Use wooden pads in the vise jaws to prevent scarring the metal.

Four cuts with a hacksaw roughly shape the point of the harpoon before it is filed to a round taper.

Fashion the head from a 5- or 6-inch length of ½-inch diameter rod. File both ends fairly smooth then use a centre punch to mark the centre at each end. Drill a ¼-inch diameter hole to a depth of 1-inch in one end. With this holed end at the bottom, grip the rod upright in the vise, and use the hacksaw to cut from the centre to one side at an angle of about 10 degrees from vertical, with the cut ending about 1 inch from the top. Repeat three more times.

Next, grip the head sideways in the vise. Use a 10-inch, double-cut file to round off the point, then finish the job with a single-cut mill file. The point and slightly rounded shoulder should slope back about 1-inch. Reverse the head in the vise and make a single cut from one side to the other, sloping the back about 30 degrees from vertical.

Place a pencil on a table and determine the head's balance point by placing it crossways on the pencil. Mark this point with a felt-tip pen and centre punch it. Drill a ¼-inch diameter hole crossways through the head, then chamfer the edges with a ⅜-inch bit. To ensure that this hole through the head is dead smooth, thread a 2-foot length of nylon parachute cord through it and dampen the centre portion with Brasso brass cleaner. As you pull the cord back and forth you will actually be able to see a slight buildup of metal on its surface.

For harpoon handles you can use wooden push-broom handles purchased at a local hardware store. They are about 50 inches long and ⅞-inch in diameter. Drill a ¼-inch diameter hole to a depth of 3 inches in one end, and into this fit a 14-inch length of ¼-inch diameter brass rod.

Use a double-cut file as a wood rasp to reduce the handle's diameter to ¾-inch for a length of 2 inches. Over this fit a 3-inch length of stainless steel tubing (or brass, if you wish).

If the tubing does not fit tightly, remove it, mix up a batch of 5-minute epoxy, coat the end of the handle with it and replace the

A band of metal tubing creates a strong joint between the harpoon handle and shaft.

The slot in the handle aids in storing the line.

tubing. Flow the remaining epoxy into the end of the tubing and then stand the handle upright in a corner and leave it overnight to cure.

I pondered filing a groove around the end of the shaft to accept an O-ring that would hold the head on the shaft, but decided instead to try Velcro on the handle. It works well enough that I never did try the O-ring.

Drill a ¼ inch-diameter hole crossways through the top of the handle, 2 inches from the end. Use the hacksaw to make two cuts down to the hole, creating a slot.

Cut a piece of the hooked portion of 2-inch wide Velcro (or two pieces 1-inch wide) long enough to completely encircle the handle just above the stainless steel band, and another for just below the slot. Cover the back of each liberally with Goop, Shoe Goo or similar flexible cement, wrap them around the handle and secure them tightly in place with masking tape. After they have cured overnight, remove the masking tape and smear some flexible cement over ½-inch of the end of a 3¾-inch length of the looped Velcro portion and press it into the lower band of hooked Velcro. Do the same at the top, but for this one increase the looped Velcro's length to 6 inches.

The harpoon head should move freely inside of the loop.

I used 30 feet of nylon parachute cord on each of the harpoons that I made. First, melt the ends with a match or lighter flame to prevent unravelling. Thread one end through the hole in the harpoon head and double the cord back 6 inches to form a loop. To close the loop use heavy nylon thread to tightly wrap the cords together for 2 inches back from the melted end. This leaves enough room that the head can rotate either way through the loop. If you have made the head longer than suggested, simply increase the loop's length accordingly.

Double the cord's other end and make a similar loop about 4 inches long overall. Coat the threaded portion of both wrapped areas with Varathane or a similar clear plastic enamel.

For storage and travel, open the two Velcro straps. Install the head on the shaft, pull the cord tight and place it in the slot, then pull it tightly back down to the shaft, wrap around it and back up to the slot.

Holding the line in preparation for harpooning.

Do this until all of the cord is wrapped end-to-end along the handle, then secure everything with the Velcro straps.

Don't wait until a halibut is hooked to ready the harpoon for use, do it before you start fishing. Unwrap the cord, but leave it folded over once in the slot and secure it with the rear Velcro strap.

To use the harpoon, pull some cord back through the groove and double it against the handle where you will be gripping it, then undo the Velcro strap and flip the cord from the slot. Remember—the only thing holding the head to the shaft is your grip on that doubled cord. Have a companion hang onto the remaining cord in order to control the harpooned halibut or hold it with your free hand. Once the head is thrust through a fish's body, releasing pressure on the cord as the shaft is withdrawn allows the head to cock sideways.

Wrapping the line for storage.

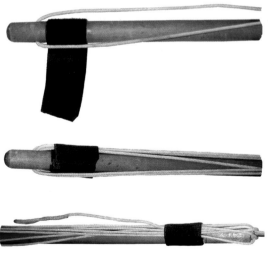

5 DRESSING THE PART

. . . .

altwater anglers often spend hours fussing with their tackle, ensuring that everything is in good condition and functioning properly. Boats, motors and trailers are inspected and lubricated, corrosion protection is applied and tire pressures checked. Safety equipment, compass, VHF radio, Global Positioning System, radar, depth sounder—virtually everything possible is checked to ensure a safe, comfortable trip. Then, likely as not, many of these conscientious people will depart without some item of clothing or sun protection, which will probably make for an uncomfortable day on the water.

Survival Suits

Many anglers swear by one-piece survival suits, while others prefer two-piece. Whichever your choice, remember that in addition to providing buoyancy these outfits also act as effective windbreakers when you are running in an open boat, especially in cool or cold weather. A hood that rolls up and stores in the collar can be a real blessing at times.

Wet Weather Gear

Despite the claims of manufacturers about the water repellent qualities of their particular brand of woven material, it's interesting to note that most fishing guides wear rubber on cloth, like the venerable Helly Hansen line. Enough said. Guests at fishing resorts can usually expect to have wet weather clothing and sur-

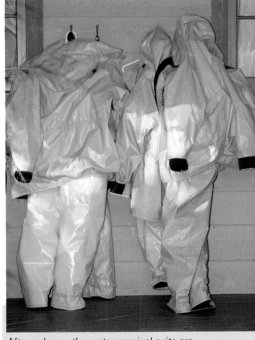

After a day on the water, survival suits are hung to dry and air out.

vival suits supplied; however, there is no guarantee that everything—or anything—will fit. Vera and I never go anywhere without our own Helly Hansen rain gear.

Hot Weather Gear

While out in a boat—especially an open boat—on those nice days that we all love, anglers are subjected to both direct sunlight from above and reflected sunlight from the water's surface, and unless protective measures are taken, one is as dangerous as the other. However, despite the well-publicized danger of skin cancer caused by excessive exposure to the sun, common summer attire on the water often consists of shorts, T-shirts, halter tops, even bathing suits. I know better than to try converting these sun worshippers, so the following is directed at readers who are interested in protecting themselves.

During warm, sunny weather the most effective sun protection is proper clothing worn in combination with sunscreen. This means footwear, socks, full-length slacks, long-sleeved shirts, wide-brimmed hats and gloves. Some clothing manufacturers actually state the Sun Protection Factor (SPF) rating on their tags, while the folks at Tilley Endurables suggest that holding an article of clothing up to the sun provides a good indication of its protectiveness. By this test, you can see that a loosely woven T-shirt is virtually useless but a tightly-woven, lightweight shirt greatly reduces light penetration.

While a straw hat might feel cool to wear, it actually offers little UV protection. A tightly woven cloth hat is superior, and most of them can be soaked with water and then worn for the added cooling effect as they dry. And though a wide-brimmed hat will protect your neck, ears and face from direct sunlight, it won't do much for reflected sunlight. A flap that drops down around the neck and ears offers a partial solution, and sunscreen will do the rest. Lightweight fingerless gloves will provide suitable protection to the wrists and backs of your hands. (I also use mine for long-distance driving during hot, sunny weather.) Even when the weather turns cooler, if the sun is out, your hands can still get burnt. You can then switch to fingerless gloves of wool, Lycra, or neoprene, and finally to standard gloves or mittens of the same materials for really chilly days.

A sunscreen's protection is limited by its Sun Protection Factor (SPF), which indicates the rate that ultraviolet (UV) rays are absorbed into the skin. SPF15 takes 15 minutes to absorb what you would experience during one minute without sunscreen, SPF30 takes 30 minutes to one minute, and so forth. Regular applications throughout the day are recommended.

People who are prone to cold sores (herpes simplex virus 1) often have breakouts if their lips get sunburnt. This is reason enough to purchase a stick of lip sunscreen and apply it often during the day. When I do get a cold sore, the best over-the-counter medication I have found is sold under the trade name Lipsorex Plus. Though horribly expensive at over $8 for a tiny tube of gel, it is most effective.

Eye Protection

A day on the water without eye protection may cause monumental headaches and adversely affect your night vision while driving. Worse, continued unprotected exposure to UV rays causes cumulative eye damage that can lead to cataracts and macular degeneration. Therefore, the claim to look for when choosing sunglasses is "100 percent UV protection." Next, ensure that the lenses are polarized to reduce and filter out horizontally reflected glare. Aviator-style glasses are popular, but wraparound models and those with side lenses offer the most protection from reflected sunlight. The final important consideration is lens colour. Grey is your best choice for all-round use on open water as it blocks out the most light.

Seasickness

Seasickness is a condition that affects some people all of the time, others only occasionally, and a lucky few not at all. (It is not to be

Rough water conditions can be expected off the West Coast.

confused with hangovers, which are self-induced afflictions that can be avoided by "clean living.") Most people relate seasickness to rough water conditions, and while this is often the case, others can handle rough water quite well until they get a whiff or two of engine exhaust or, in my own case, excessive cigarette smoke.

My wife loves to fish but is susceptible to seasickness. As a result, she researched this subject thoroughly then set about trying various tactics to relieve the condition. Over-the-counter oral medicaments didn't do much for her, but Sea-Band wristbands work quite well. Our greatest problem with wrist bands has been keeping them on hand for she is forever giving them away to friends who suffer from motion sickness while travelling in cars or airplanes. (Most have reported positive results.)

Something else Vera learned was to control the visual situation by keeping her eyes focussed on the distant horizon. This has worked for her off the west coast of the Island and on Milbanke Sound on the central coast, which also experiences those high rollers from the open Pacific. She still got a tad greenish of hue but was able to tough it out rather than cause us to run in for calmer water.

As Janice Stefanyk is also prone to a tinge of green while in rolling seas, she too did some research and recommends that anyone with the least bit of motion sickness problems should always go prepared for the worst. Start by taking a product like Bonomine or Dramamine at least 24 hours in advance. She has also used a herbal product called Cocculine, which does the job despite lumpy water conditions, and it has none of the usual sleepy side effects.

This, then, is the secret: experiment until you find something that works for you. It might be as simple as taking an over-the-counter medication like Dramamine, Bonine or Marezine, or require a prescribed tranquillizer or nervous system depressant from your physician. If something like Sea-Bands or Bio Bands work for you, purchase an extra set or two to keep in reserve. There are also herbal remedies, acupuncture devices, and homeopathic products that work well for many people.

PART TWO

6 WHERE TO FISH

It doesn't matter where you fish around Vancouver Island, you might put this beauty in your boat.

*B*eing properly equipped is only one facet of the "secret" to becoming a successful halibut angler. Much will depend on preparation, and that starts with doing your homework beforehand to determine the best combination of known tidal conditions and average weather conditions for a given location. This means sitting down with a current tide guide to look for tides that have the least amount of movement between high and low. But this is also where the value of a fishing diary becomes evident because by keeping records you can plan future trips. If you don't have a diary, there is no time like the present to start. All you require is a steno pad or shirt-pocket notebook in which to make daily entries. By periodically transferring your daily notes onto a computer or into an annual diary, you will create a permanent record that will be worth its weight in gold when it comes to trip planning.

Halibut are migratory, so the time to fish for them is when they are known to be most abundant in a particular area. Finding this out is simply a matter of asking at a local tackle shop or sorting through the "Area Reports" and articles found in past issues of *Island Fisherman* magazine. Some areas noted for being dependable halibut hotspots are fairly far offshore, so a properly equipped boat of suitable size and seaworthiness will be required; others are relatively close to launch sites that are easily accessible by road, making them ideal for smaller boats with a less impressive array of electronic navigation devices. However, if you have the location and timing down pat but the tides are wrong or the wind is blowing hard, plan on doing something else because you won't be bottom fishing. Wind is really the only part of this equation that depends on luck. While certain periods of the year are known to be prone to heavy winds, you simply never know when something unusual—or unseasonable—might crop up.

Determining the locations where halibut should be found is relatively simple. They prefer a fairly level sand or gravel bottom with structures that provide protection from strong tidal currents but also create conditions that attract food sources. The ocean is filled with such places, so all you have to do is find them. Some of these underwater structures are massive, like La Pèrouse Bank offshore from Barkley Sound or Taylor Bank in Queen Charlotte Strait, while others might be little more than a kitchen-table-sized indentation on an otherwise flat bottom, a sudden drop-off, the base of a pinnacle, a cluster of large rocks—basically any combination that provides halibut with both comfort and food.

Unfortunately, finding this type of potential habitat is often the easy part. As halibut are migratory, there is no guarantee that you will actually find them present in this ideal location at the particular time you have chosen to go fishing. Or even if the bottom is blanketed with halibut, that the wind and tidal currents will be favourable enough to permit bottom fishing. Or that the halibut will be interested in your offering once you do get it down there. As the old sage said, "That's why it's called fishing and not catching."

Fifty years ago locating halibut grounds used to involve using marine charts, a compass and triangulation if you happened to be close enough to shore to pick out landmarks or buoys. The introduction of sonar units small enough for use in recreational fishing boats suddenly provided vital information about the water depths, and when Loran

Vera Jones hooked this 40-pounder about 20 feet below the *Silver Fox* while lowering her leadhead jig.

came along, locating and relocating known hotspots became much easier. The more recent introduction of Global Positioning Systems (GPS) has made things easier still. However, don't throw away your marine charts just yet as they can still provide a "picture" of where suitable bottom conditions, banks and shoals are located. This is not only the sort of information that makes going to a new area much easier, it can also be used to explore potential halibut grounds adjacent to your regular fishing area.

The depths at which halibut are caught usually depend on a range of variables. I have caught them at just over 500 feet in upper Queen Charlotte Strait and watched Murray Gardham hook that previously-mentioned 138-pounder off the dock in Double Bay in about 40 feet of water. Ian Andersen tells of a young fellow in Port Hardy who got a 127-pounder while Buzz Bombing off the Seagate Wharf in 20 feet of water, and Martin Paish, former Northern Operations Manager for the Oak Bay Marine Group, recalls watching halibut feeding just beneath the surface off Langara Island. I recall Vera hooking a 40-pounder about 20 feet below the *Silver Fox* while lowering her jig (the depth sounder read over 300 feet), and many of us have had halibut take lures that were being retrieved and were well up off the bottom. Nevertheless, if you want to attract halibut, 99 times out of 100 you had better have your bait or lure on or near the bottom, no matter how deep the water.

Many millions of years ago when Vancouver Island separated from the mainland, it was far from a clean break. As a result, although there are some fairly flat, featureless areas in the Strait of Georgia and in Queen Charlotte Strait, for the most part the entire Inside Passage is a mass of rocky, uneven, unforgiving, tackle-grabbing bottom. Fortunately, halibut do quite well in these surroundings—as do tackle manufacturers and distributors.

Off the west coast of Vancouver Island halibut fishing is a game of pluses

A common saying of the west coast of Vancouver Island is: "If you don't like the weather, wait five minutes." This is why it is wise to always keep an eye on weather conditions.

and minuses. Offshore fishing out of popular destinations like Winter Harbour, Zeballos, Tahsis, Tofino, Ucluelet, Bamfield and Port Renfrew means you are exposed to high swells rolling in from the open Pacific, and the constant up-down-up-down causes a lot of queasy stomachs. Adding a cross-chop to provide some side-to-side and back-and-forth to the up-down-up-down then blending in occasional whiffs of engine exhaust is almost guaranteed to have pasty-green-hued people hanging over the gunwales. On the plus side, the overall bottom found along the Island's west coast tends to be a fairly gentle slope from the continental shelf to the shoreline, with several large, offshore banks looming up at various locations. Much of the bottom on top of and surrounding these banks is blanketed with sand and gravel, which makes for relatively easy, snag-free jigging and bait fishing. Once closer inshore, however, there are pinnacles, rock piles, shoals and islands, and suddenly the bottom is nowhere near as forgiving when it comes to lowering expensive tackle into the depths. In fact, it becomes very similar to what anglers on the Island's east coast accept as typical bottom fishing conditions.

7 FISHING TACTICS

*I*n the old days many of the anglers who caught halibut while they were trolling, mooching or drift-jigging for salmon were fishing deep with wire lines and diving planers, the use of which required heavyweight rods and reels. The use of those pool-cue-sized rods and winch-like reels loaded with 60- to 100-pound-test nylon monofilament was tiring, and it was obvious overkill for halibut weighing less than 50 pounds. But many halibut that were hooked by moochers and drift jiggers were lost, which probably accounted for tales of huge chinooks that had broken off after wild battles

Bill von Brendel hooked this 45-pounder while trolling a small squid hoochie off Ucluelet.

during which the fish stayed deep and never surfaced. Those who did land their fish often got their pictures in local newspapers along with write-ups in which the angler admitted that there was more luck than skill involved in boating the fish.

Small cruisers like this Hourston Glascraft are popular with West Coast saltwater anglers.

Trolling

After downriggers caught on with recreational anglers in the 1970s, the number of incidental encounters with halibut increased accordingly and so did the numbers of

75

Tomic Plugs are a good choice when deep trolling for halibut, but you might want to pinch that hook barb just in case a salmon hits . . . or a fisheries enforcement officer arrives on the scene.

fish that were landed successfully. Anglers discovered two important things: halibut—even sizeable ones—can be handled with salmon-weight tackle and they are actually strong fighters. They are nowhere near as fast-swimming as a chinook salmon but pound for pound just as strong. Before long, some anglers started intentionally fishing for halibut by simply downrigging deep and slow, usually with plugs or large herring, and their efforts were rewarded with increased catches. Sooke fishing guide Mark Grant (Mark Grant's Salmon Charters) has been going after halibut with salmon gear for several years. During March and April, weather permitting, he downrigs with a revolving flasher, about five feet of leader and either a whole herring or anchovy or a large strip. One of his favourite stretches is along the shelf bordering the shoreline between Otter Point and Point No Point, where it averages 30 to 80 feet deep over a sandy bottom, though he does fish deeper on occasion. "It takes longer to land your fish than if you used heavy tackle," Mark told me, "but if you don't rush things it can be done. The nice thing is that while you're fishing close to the bottom, you're just as likely to pick up a salmon." That Mark has landed halibut to 170 pounds is proof his system works and that, when properly used, salmon tackle will handle even those big barn doors.

Some anglers use a downrigger to fish the bottom while drifting, an option when the tide is running too fast for jigging. This is best accomplished with bait, but don't overlook trying a plug. Being buoyant, plugs won't sink to

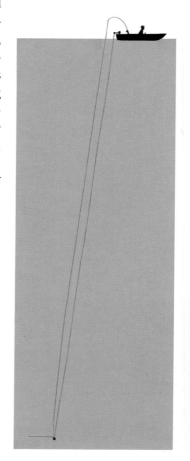

Slow trolling with a downrigger allows you to cover more water

The result of using a Rhys Davis teaser head and strip while trolling for Ucluelet halibut.

the bottom, and there is usually enough current that they will wobble enticingly.

Larry Stefanyk recalls that the first time he ever trolled for halibut was while fishing out of Ucluelet with guide Bill von Brendel. When bottom-bouncing with salmon belly on a spreader bar didn't produce, von Brendel suggested that they pull their gear and try trolling, pointing out that they could cover more area that way and stand a better chance of locating fish. "We headed for totally different structure," Larry said. "Bill was looking for bottom that had a drop-off but would run for a half mile or so before changing and not too deep—150 feet seemed to be the magic number."

Once satisfied with what he saw on the sounder, von Brendel rigged two of his Shimano salmon rods with Hot Spot Flashers and 42-inch leaders of 40-pound-test monofilament. Attached to one was a blue Rhys Davis Teaser Head with a large herring strip and to the other a small blue/green hoochie. After lowering the cannonballs to the bottom, von Brendel slipped the motor into gear and started letting out more downrigger cable as the boat moved forward. When he finally stopped letting out cable, the line gauge read 175 feet and the cable was at an angle of well over 45 degrees. Placing the rods in the stern-mounted holders, he cautioned Larry that any takes would be very gentle—the rod would make only two or three soft bounces—but in all likelihood there would be a halibut on.

No more than five minutes later the tip of the rod with the strip barely dipped three times. Von Brendel quickly plucked the rod from its holder and handed it to Larry with instructions to reel up any slack in the line, explaining that he would then drop the cannonball to pop the line clip. It went just like clockwork and Larry found himself fighting the first halibut he had ever hooked while intentionally trolling for them. It weighed a respectable 45 pounds and was the first of four they took very quickly before heading home.

Larry also mentioned a slow-trolling tactic that he learned from Jim Walls while fishing out of Walls Fish Camp at Ocean Falls on the central coast. After running out to Milbanke Sound, they rigged with standard halibut gear—a 6-foot rod and a reel filled with 100-pound-test braided TUF line. On the terminal end were a 1-pound sinker and a no. 5 circle hook on a 5-foot leader of 100-pound-test nylon monofilament. After skewering a herring on the hook, they secured it there with a piece of salmon belly.

While Walls kept the motor in gear, holding the boat in position so the terminal tackle would drop straight down, he told Larry to free-spool his sinker to the bottom about 200 feet below. Once the sinker was on the sandy bottom, Walls slipped the motor into neutral. As the boat drifted, he told Larry to continue releasing line periodically in order to keep his sinker on the bottom with the bait floating above it. When Larry detected a bite, Walls instructed him to feed out a bit more slack in order to give the fish time to take the bait. After a few moments, Larry reeled in the slack, confirmed that the fish was still there, and set the hook. They returned that afternoon with their limit of halibut plus a few lingcod.

"No jigging was required," Larry explained, "but there is a bit more reeling. That's why having a reel with lots of line is necessary. And there is no reason why that same tactic won't produce on the west coast of the Island. Or anywhere else where there's a fairly flat, sandy or gravel bottom."

Bottom Bouncing With Bait or Lures

If fishing bait with a fishfinder setup or a spreader bar, always control the terminal tackle's drop to the bottom with light thumb pressure on

To free a snagged line:

With gel-spun line, either braided or single strand, the lack of stretch often makes it possible to feel a potentially immoveable snag. As there will be pressure building on the line from the boat's drift, immediately place your thumb on the spooled line and apply pressure as you flip the reel into free-spool. Failure to apply thumb pressure will result in a monumental backlash as the spool suddenly starts spinning. After it's in free-spool, lighten up on the thumb pressure and feed out enough line until it goes slack, then flip back into gear and quickly lift the rod tip until you can barely feel tension. Shake the rod tip vigorously, then lower it again to feel whether the hook has come free. This technique won't work every time but does often enough to make it your first response. If it doesn't come free, your next response should be to loosen the line enough that you can make several wraps around the wooden handle of a gaff or fish club, then back the boat "upstream" from the line of drift and try a steady pull. Never wrap the line around your hand—with or without gloves—for the results can be painfully disastrous.

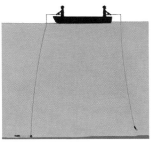

Keep your lines as close to vertical as possible.

When a tidal current moves the boat along, hopping your jig along the bottom will increase your fishing time.

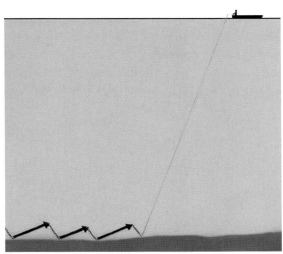

the reel's revolving spool. If it drops too quickly, the bait—being lighter than the sinker–will almost always double back up and wrap around the main line. Once on the bottom, lift the weight occasionally so everything makes short hops rather than drags, which will hang up more often.

Whether bottom-bouncing with bait or lures, the lines should always be maintained as close to vertical as possible. There is usually some drift, however, due to tidal currents and wind, but this is not a problem as long as the drift speed permits you to continue feeling the bottom by occasionally feeding out a bit of line. Once the line bellies and lifts the terminal tackle off the bottom, it's time to use motor power to adjust the boat's position in relation to the lines. Once a tide starts running in earnest, of course, it's time to go salmon fishing, whale watching, or simply stop for a while.

There are two ways to fish bait. With the active method you hold the rod and wait for a bite, then set the hook when you think the time is right. With the passive method you simply place the rod in a holder, monitor the rod for any sign of a bite, and then remove it from the holder. Better yet in most cases is to let a fish chew on the bait until it hooks itself before you pick up the rod. This tactic has gained in popularity since circle hooks have come into common use by recreational anglers, and many guides claim that it's the best method to use with clients who are inexperienced at halibut fishing.

If fishing a top-rigged jig, the standard tactic is to hop it along the bottom, lifting it about 6-12 inches, with occasional longer lifts of up to 2 feet. This can be rhythmic, erratic, or a combination of both. The idea is to keep the hoochie in motion to provide visual attraction and the lure pounding on the bottom to create sound. (It's a fact that well-used pipe jigs are usually splayed out at their bottom end.) How fast to lift a jig is as debatable as how far, but most anglers practice the slow-lift-fast-drop method.

Handlining

On my first trip with handliner Ian Andersen he told me, "I can actually feel what's happening down there. I can feel the impact of a Lucky Jig hitting bottom, and I can actually feel the hook flopping around. If I don't, I haul it in and clean it off. I can tell whether the bottom is hard or soft, coming up or dropping away. You can actually feel the hookup when a fish hits, and you can retrieve about five times faster than with a reel." Ian's best fish caught on a handline weighed a very respectable 267 pounds.

Lucky Jigs, originally developed by James Darkin of Campbell River around 1980, were popularized and improved upon by the late Mike Robert of Comox.

Mike Robert stressed the importance of handlining during high or low slack tides: "You've got to have slack water. If you can't find any, head someplace where you know the bottom is good. That way, if you drag along the bottom, it's no big deal. If you try where the bottom's bad, you've had it. My lures are designed to be fished standing up; if they tip on their side they hook bottom just like the rest."

He was also adamant about how they should be fished: "Thumping a Lucky Jig on the bottom attracts fish. I thump three times, wait for five seconds, then thump three more times. If that doesn't attract any attention, I pull it up a bit and flutter it around, then lower it and reaffirm the bottom. You don't have to jerk it up and down like a cod jig. In addition to the thumping sound, it rotates and that eight-sided finish reflects light, and the hoochie is pulsing in and out."

With the strong line that is advocated for handlining, what do you do if you hang up on bottom? According to Ian, you act immediately or face the prospect of losing everything. "Never try to hold it with your hand," he said. "Take a few wraps around a wooden fish club or gaff handle, then run the boat back up on your line of drift until you're pulling from the opposite direction. If it doesn't come loose, take some wraps around a deck cleat and use the boat to pull it free."

Drift-Jigging

A common practice while drift-jig-ging is to cast well upstream from the line of drift, then allow the lure to sink while controlling the free-spooling reel with light thumb pressure. Once you feel bottom, engage the spool, reel in a few feet of line, and then let it sink to the bottom again. As the lure passes under the boat, start feeding line out occasionally, so you can still feel bottom. Once at an angle of 15 degrees or so away

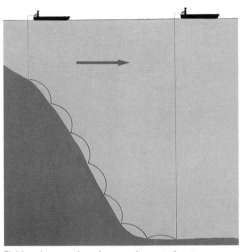

Fishing down a slope is a good way to locate feeding halibut.

from the drifting boat, let the line's pull lift the lure up from the bottom a bit more, then start reeling in at a slow, steady rate. Once the lure is about halfway back to the surface, reel in quickly and cast again. Halibut will occasionally swim up off the bottom after a lure, and some will follow almost to the surface before biting.

If there is little or no drift, simply drop the lure straight down from the rod tip. Hold your rod so the tip is just touching the water, and con-trol the spool's rotation with light thumb pressure against the line. If the lure hesitates during the drop, this signals that a fish has taken it. Jam your thumb down on the spool as you lift the rod tip to set the hook, while at the same time rotating the reel handle to engage the spool. It could be a tiny rockfish, a large chinook or coho, or even a halibut. You won't know until the hook is set.

If the lure sinks all the way down without being intercepted, as soon as you feel it touch bottom, jam your thumb down on the spool as you rotate the reel handle to engage the spool. Then lift the rod tip sharply as if setting the hook. Every once in a while that's precisely what you will be doing—it's almost as though a halibut was down there waiting with its mouth open.

The first time I tried a then brand new Yellowtail Zzinger, Vera and I were fishing with Murray Gardham off Stubbs Island in Blackfish Sound. Murray had lowered a foot-long whole herring to the bottom, and I had rigged Vera with her favourite leadhead jig trailing a pink Delta Jumbo Tail. I was using a Fenwick 10½-foot graphite mooching rod with an Ambassadeur 6500 loaded with 20-pound-test Berkley Trilene. Murray watched quietly as I tied on the 4½-inch long Zzinger and dropped it over the side.

Finally he asked, "Just what in hell do you expect to catch on that?"

At this precise moment I felt the lure hit bottom, so engaged the reel and lifted the rod into a rather alarming bow. "A halibut," I replied calmly as I felt the fish start to streak off. And it was a halibut—a 35-pounder. I have since hooked other halibut on a Yellowtail Zzinger but never quite as swiftly.

While heading out from Double Bay Resort the following day to fish in the same area, I stopped our boat at the bay's mouth and used a white, 1½-inch long Zzinger to catch a couple of small rockfish and greenling to cut up for bait. As we started the run toward Stubbs Island, it became obvious that the water was just rough enough to be uncomfortable, whereupon Vera suggested that, as she had noticed calm water on the other side of the "Blow Hole," we should run through that narrow, rocky channel between Hanson Island and the Plumper Islands and give it a try.

I had never heard of a halibut being caught there so my heart wasn't really in it. Rather than re-rig, I simply left the tiny Zzinger on and dropped it down about 200 feet to the smooth, sandy bottom—and promptly hooked an 18-pound chicken. As it turned out, it was the only halibut of the day for the resort, which meant I had to endure constant harassment from the other guests about relying on Vera to guide me.

Slopes

Although halibut are often caught on top of small humps and larger banks during slack tides, the slopes leading up to them can also be productive. And don't overlook any flat benches running along the side of a slope, no matter how wide, for halibut are often found on them. Whether they are using them as ambush cover or actually feeding on them is anyone's guess, but they do use them.

Fishing down a slope is ideal for leadhead jigs, which can be jumped and swum with little danger of hanging up. I often leave my reel in free spool while doing this, so I can release line as required to maintain the bottom. This means my thumb is always on the spool, and I have hold of the reel handle so that, if a fish bites, the spool can be engaged as the hook is set.

Ken Jenkins suggests that catches can be increased by fish-

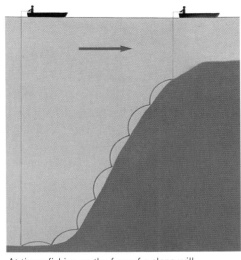

At times fishing up the face of a slope will generate bites but there is a greater potential for snags.

ing up the sloping face of a drop-off on its upstream side. If, for example, your chart shows the bottom at 600 feet and rising to a shoal at 200 feet, start fishing at about 300 feet and work up the slope. Halibut often feed actively up to 50 or 60 feet below the crest, so be prepared to hit fish from depths of about 250 feet on up. However, the possibility of hooking bottom is far greater fishing up a slope than when fishing down, so this tactic works best with top-rigged jigs or leadheads. Avoid trying it with a spreader bar as there is simply too much gear that can hang up. Use gel-spun line and keep it as close to vertical as possible so you can feel any obstructions as they are encountered. But quite often just dropping the rod tip and giving it a vigorous shake is all that's required to free the lure.

Indentations

If you find a small indentation in the bottom, mark it on the GPS. Once while I was fishing with Mike Robert near Cracroft Point in Blackfish Sound, things had been slow and the incoming tide was starting to build. We had only 20 minutes or so left before we would have to pull up, when Mike suddenly yelped, "There's a hole! There's a fish!" And as he reefed up on his handline, he reached out and quickly hit the waypoint button on his GPS. The 30-pounder came in fairly quickly and I did the honours with the harpoon.

Afterwards Mike jabbed his finger on the marine chart. "Look! That hole doesn't even show," he said accusingly, "but it's there. Let's see if we can find it again."

Back in the 1990s you could not always depend upon pinpoint location with a GPS because that was the way the military wanted it, but on this occasion our luck held and he relocated the hole right away. Mike figured it was about 6 feet deep and 100 feet long, and at the speed we were drifting we wouldn't have much time to probe it with our lures, but he dropped his Lucky Jig and I my Halibut Spinnow (I was using rod and reel). We both connected, Mike with a 28-pounder and I with a 25, all because he had the sense to reach out immediately and mark that waypoint. It's a good habit to get into.

Rock Piles and Pinnacles

Although a rock pile or pinnacle is considered ideal lingcod and rock-fish habitat, any flat bottom surrounding the base of one of these structures will appeal to halibut because the tidal currents create back eddies that stir up the food sources. For this reason, the best place to fish them is on the downstream side.

Fighting Your Halibut

At times, hauling a halibut to the surface is about as thrilling as trying to crank up a bucketful of concrete, but some fish can—and do—surprise us. While fishing with an early prototype Halibut Spinnow, I had an 85-pounder that ran 100 yards after it was hooked in 300 feet of

Choon Fong making good use of a fighting belt.

water. I had only four or five wraps of line left on my reel when it turned back and came grudgingly up toward the boat, then sounded and ran about the same amount of line out again. This went on for the better part of 45 minutes, and I was like a whipped puppy after it was finally subdued. Ken Jenkins, who has probably seen thousands of halibut caught over his years as a fishing guide, said that it had fought much harder than normal. He then added the comment that the hardest-fighting fish are usually in the 60- to 100-pound range. I believe him.

The "best" way to fight a halibut depends entirely on what size and type of boat you are fishing from. Standing upright so you are balanced with your feet spread comfortably apart provides the most effective stance for lifting the rod, then reeling in as the tip is lowered and repeating the process—pump-crank-lower reel, pump-crank. . . . If you are wearing a fighting belt, all the better as the slot in the gimballed rod handle will serve as a fulcrum point and also prevent the reel's weight from twisting the handle in your grip.

While lifting, you should stop the rod handle between 50 and 60 degrees from horizontal. In this way you will be lifting with the rod butt and central portion rather than the tip. Reel the line in as you lower the rod tip as far down as is comfortable then stop reeling as you lift the rod once more. If the reel's drag slips, apply enough thumb pressure to stop it. You should never start adjusting the drag at this point—too tight and the hook might tear loose or the line break, and too loose might result in a glorious bird's nest of line exploding from your reel. More halibut are probably lost because of fiddling with the drag than for any other reason.

If fishing from a small boat—anything under 16 feet with a wide hull—you should remain seated for the sake of safety. This is especially the case if there is wave action that would make standing difficult at the best of times, never mind while trying to handle an excited halibut. Some anglers find that tucking the rod handle under an armpit is most comfortable, while others opt for pushing the handle butt against one hip. Seated with the rod positioned in this way, you can't usually reach as far down with the rod tip, especially if there is a guard rail on the gunwale, but you should still observe the 50 to 60 degrees of lift to avoid breaking the tip section.

If a halibut proves too heavy to move up off the bottom, the standard remedy is to decrease the angle of lift by running the boat away from the fish, preferably toward shallower water. This way you will not

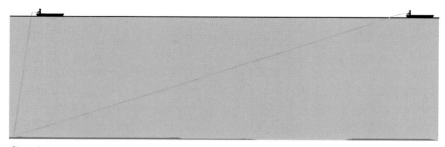

Changing the angle of pull is often the key to handling large, stubborn halibut.

be attempting what is essentially a dead lift at 90 degrees from horizontal. The more angle the better though, of course, this will depend on the amount of line you have available. For example, if the fish is down 300 feet and you have 200 yards of line on your reel, you can decrease the angle to about 40 degrees. If you have 300 yards, you can decrease it to about 20 degrees. In this case, the fish will often follow the line of pull, and there have been several catches recorded where the anglers have gone ashore and coaxed large halibut right up onto the beach to land them.

Releasing

The move toward releasing large fish started to gain popularity around the late 1990s, though some anglers had been practicing it long before then, having realized that such large halibut (and lingcod) were females of prime breeding age. You may call me cynical if you will, but I find

Releasing a small halibut is relatively easy but larger fish can pose a few problems.

that those who advocate loudest for releasing huge halibut are usually anglers or guides who fish for them often and, as a result, see a lot of large ones caught. So I don't have a problem with a 200-pounder being kept if the lucky angler who just finished derricking it up beside the boat is on his or her only one- or two-day halibut trip of the year, especially since there are commercial halibut fishermen up and down the West Coast who

A gaff hook is handy for unhooking fish that are being released.

take great delight in catching fish that have that kind of weight because they get paid by the pound. And they catch more than one or two per year. A lot more.

So release or keep? That's entirely up to the person who has caught it.

If a fish is bleeding from the gills, its chances for survival are extremely limited so you should opt for keeping it. If the fish appears to be uninjured other than the hole made by the hook, decide beforehand what you are going to do and how. If it has swallowed a baited hook, simply cut the line as close to the jaws as possible. If it is hooked in the jaw and you can see the hook, use pliers to try backing it out. It might be necessary to crush the barb at least part way flat—which might be easier said than done, depending upon the fish's cooperation. If you can grip the line, pull it back tightly toward the fish's tail so the hook rotates in its jaw, then slide the point of a gaff hook inside the hook's bend and jerk it loose. This is also the best method for removing the treble hook on a top-rigged jig or lure. Some anglers carry small bolt cutters, which make short work of cutting a hook shank.

Landing

In a small boat things will get dicey when it comes time to land a halibut because a serious judgement call must be made about whether one or more of you should stand up. Remaining seated is always the safest option, but a word of warning—move to opposite sides of the boat in order to maintain balance. If the person harpooning or gaffing the fish is right-handed and the fish is on the right side of the boat, shift as far left on your seat as possible. This

Corey Hayes uses a gaff hook to land this nice halibut.

will give your partner room to reach out and grab the line in his left hand in order to guide the fish's head into position, leaving his right hand free to harpoon or gaff it. And if the fish suddenly streaks off, you will have a better chance of regaining control of the situation without having your rod crash into your partner.

In a former life, Ralph Shaw and I used to do a dog-and-pony act at outdoors shows for a major whisky distiller. In it we covered all facets of freshwater and saltwater recreational fishing, but we quickly determined that our most popular presentation was "Bottom Fishing." During the opening remarks I would always ask for a show of hands of those who had caught their first halibut while fishing from a boat in the 12- to 16-foot range. There would always be a show of hands, usually up to a half dozen or more, whereupon I would ask how many had gaffed said halibut and promptly hauled it into the boat. The same number of hands would usually go up again, after which I would ask how many of them quickly realized that this had been an extremely bad move. And again most hands rose into the air. I would then ask each one to tell the audience what had happened. The responses included trashed tackle boxes, broken rods, entire fishing outfits knocked right out of the boat, several sprains and a few broken bones. The amazing thing was that most of the fish involved with this mayhem turned out to be less than 60 pounds.

I am sure that anyone who attended those presentations would never again consider lifting a live halibut of any size into a small boat without first disabling it. The problem is not so much the size of the fish as the fact that halibut are difficult to stun. One well-placed whack on the head with a fish club will disable a salmon of any size, but repeated blows on the head of a halibut seem to do nothing more than annoy it.

Ian Andersen tells of drifting near the Gordon Islands north of Port Hardy and hearing the faint sound of voices over his boat's idling diesel engine. After scanning the waters of Goletas Channel for a few seconds, he spotted a small boat off in the distance. Ducking into the cabin for his binoculars, he saw that it was a couple of 12- or 13-year-old boys. "They were out there in a 14-foot riveted aluminum boat," Ian said. "One kid was sitting on top of the outboard and the other was straddling the bow. Every once in awhile something would wave around in the middle of the boat, and I finally realized it was the centre seat.

"One of them had hooked a 150-pound halibut and managed to get it up beside the boat. They didn't have a gaff, so with the skill and cunning that only young boys possess, they both got on one side of the boat so they were almost shipping water, got the halibut's head over the gunwale and pulled it into the boat with them. When it proceeded to flop around, one of the first things to go was the centre seat—the rivets sheared on one side so the other side acted like a hinge. They didn't even have anything to hit it with, so they had got as far out of its way as they could. But with the seat gone, the thin sides of the boat started folding inward and it was taking on water. Fortunately, we managed to get to them before they went down, but they were two scared boys. We even managed to get their fish on board, but that poor old boat was a total write-off."

Not everyone fishes from small boats, of course. Over the years I have seen many halibut of up to 80-plus pounds bouncing around on the wide aft deck of Ian's 40-foot *Silver Fox*. But everybody made a point to stand well back until he picked an opportune moment to step in and swing the back end of his striker gaff against the fish's head and stun it long enough to lift it into the fish box. Yes, he obviously knows where to hit them for maximum effect.

Harpooning

Although halibut under 50 pounds can be netted, most anglers usually opt to harpoon or gaff them, even fairly small fish. Properly used, a toggle-style harpoon is very efficient. If you are right-handed, position yourself on the angler's right side so you have complete control over the harpoon handle. Meanwhile, the angler must try to line the fish up sideways to the boat but might not be able to accomplish this by leading it with the rod tip. In some cases the harpooner can reach out and grasp the line then pull the fish's head in close enough to drive the harpoon home.

You don't *throw* a harpoon like a spear. Simply line up the head's point right behind the gill collar, slightly to one side or the other of the lateral line in

This relatively small harpoon head is called a "dart."

X marks the spot to hit
a halibut with the
harpoon head.

order to miss the spine, and then drive the head completely through the
fish's body with one thrust. Going right through is important; otherwise, the head will probably pull back out. When you withdraw the
handle, the head will slip free from the steel shaft and turn sideways,
effectively stopping it when it comes up against the fish's body. Usually
at this point the halibut will make a run so the angler must be ready to
handle the rod accordingly. He should not add pressure to the reel spool
but just let the harpooner handle the fish with the rope and then reel in
the slack line as necessary.

Bleeding a halibut by slashing the gills guarantees improved flesh quality.

To make a hog-tier hook:

Many years ago I fashioned the first of several hog-tier hooks from a no. 16 shark hook and about 8 feet of parachute cord.

Begin by folding 3 inches of cord back on one end and binding it for 2 inches with heavy nylon thread to create a 1-inch loop. Fold an 8-inch length to form a 4-inch loop. Bind both ends to the hook shank for 1 inch, leaving a 3-inch loop extending beyond the hook eye. After threading the tag end of the cord through the end loop and the hook eye, tie the tag end into a simple hard knot to prevent it from pulling back through the eye.

To use the hog-tier hook, open the end loop, slip it over the halibut's tail and pull it tight around the wrist. Pull 2 or 3 feet of the tag end through the hook eye, and then place the hook point inside the halibut's mouth. Pulling steadily on the tag end sets the hook in the fish's jaw as the tail is drawn up, forcing the body into a bow. Maintaining pressure on the line, double it back around the tail wrist, then grip the three lines tightly together as the tag end is threaded through the hook loop, pulled tight then tied off. This entire operation takes only a few seconds. This hog-tier has proved handy for subduing halibut that were too large for the fish box, and on occasion we have even used it in the water for hog-tying a halibut before lifting it into the boat.

Gay Gair with a hog-tied 60-pounder taken with a handline near Port Hardy.

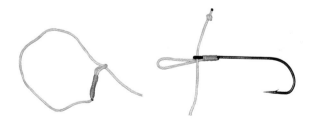

A Hog-tier Hook makes quick work of immobilizing a halibut.

If you have harpooned the fish on the right side of its spine, the head will probably have gone through some of the vital organs. The fish will lose blood rapidly, and once weakened will be easier—meaning safer—to handle. Pull the fish beside the boat and use a gaff hook through the lower jaw to lift its head slightly above the water. A halibut's brain is located behind the left eye (farthest from its mouth), and two or three heavy blows should stun it. However, never assume it is dead, for unlike salmon, halibut have a disconcerting habit of recovering.

No matter what size your fish is, the best thing to do at this point is to tether and bleed it. (This is certainly the safest step to follow with anything above chicken size.) Slide the stiffened end of a tether under a gill cover and out through the mouth, and then lift the fish's head close enough that you can sever the gill arches near the throat (don't cut through the V-shaped isthmus of the throat itself). Adjust the rope so the fish's head is out of the water and then tie it to a cleat. A halibut will bleed to death fairly fast, and the quality of its flesh will be much improved over that of a fish that isn't bled.

If a fish must be brought into the boat before it has bled to death, it should be hog-tied. This is accomplished by fastening a tight loop of a tether rope around the wrist of the fish's tail and then half-hitching it twice. Push the stiff end of the tether under a gill cover and out through the mouth, then pull it through until the fish forms a curve. Double the rope back to the tail, make two or three more wraps and two half hitches around the wrist. Tied in this manner, if the halibut happens to recover, it will be unable to move. If fishing from a small boat, hog-tying even small fish will prevent them from creating a disturbance.

A classic example of what could happen to an angler who doesn't follow the bleed and/or hog-tie rule occurred a few years ago when two fishing buddies from Victoria launched their boat at Sooke and set out for Swiftsure Bank. It was a great day for halibut fishing and they were rewarded with their limit, the last one weighing about 70 pounds. They bonked it while it was still in the water, then ran a line through its gills and mouth and secured it to a cleat before they lifted it into the boat.

Later, after dropping his friend off at home with his two fish, the boat's owner headed for home, towing it through downtown Victoria. He was almost at the city centre when he noticed that car horns were honking and pedestrians were pointing at him and frantically waving their arms. Puzzled, he pulled over and got out to investigate. It was quite a sight. His 70-pounder had revived, jumped over the gunwale and was hanging against the side of his boat, flapping wildly.

Now our angler was at an age where he simply couldn't lift the halibut back into the boat. Fortunately, from the small crowd that had formed to watch the excitement, a gentlemen stepped forward, removed his suit jacket and tie, and easily lifted the halibut back into the boat as the crowd applauded his efforts. One can but wonder how this good Samaritan explained the condition of his clothes when he arrived home.

While this story had a happy ending, had the rope broken or the cleat pulled loose, this wouldn't have been the case. The moral, of course, is to make sure that halibut are dispatched properly by bleeding them. And if you are lifting a fish into the boat, hog-tie it—just in case.

Using a Flying Gaff

I was introduced to flying gaffs the first time I went out in a Codfather Charters boat because all of their guides favour using a shark hook flying gaff over a harpoon. These gaffs are economical, take up little space,

Ken Jenkins gaffs a chicken while another is suspended from the gunwale to bleed.

and are quite dependable when properly set into the head or shoulder of a halibut. Most Codfather's boats carry at least two or three, so in the event that a large fish—150 pounds or more—is brought to the surface, more than one gaff can be used if necessary.

A flying gaff can also be used to suspend a fish from the gunwale while it bleeds or to move a fish around once it is in the boat.

Shooting Halibut

The rule for shooting halibut is "don't!" The *British Columbia Tidal Waters Sport Fishing Guide* states explicitly in the General Restrictions: "It is illegal to use stones, clubs, firearms, explosives or chemicals to molest, injure or kill fish." Shooting was a fairly common practice in the past, and there were even a few horror stories about anglers shooting at fish after they were in the boat—and missing. It wouldn't surprise me to learn that a few anglers still shoot large fish, but aside from being illegal, shooting is not really necessary.

Halibut tagging is part of a study being conducted by the International Pacific Halibut Commission.

The IPHC Halibut Tagging Program

The International Pacific Halibut Commission (IPHC) has an ongoing program to tag and monitor halibut migrations and mortality. Their plastic-coded wire tags are normally attached to the top (dark) gill cover but they may be found on or near the head or some other part of the body. Each tag has a unique number and the letters IPHC printed on it. Anglers are urged to keep all tagged halibut. Remove the tag and record the number along with the date caught, location and depth, the fish's length and sex. Mail this information and the tag to: International Pacific Halibut Commission, PO Box 95009, Seattle, WA, USA, 98145-2009 (phone (206) 634-1838). There is a small reward for your efforts—$5 or a baseball cap—but your main reward will be in assisting with IPHC's research.

IPHC Halibut Length-Weight Table

The following chart shows halibut length in inches and corresponding weight in pounds, based on the International Pacific Halibut Commission table.

Length	Weight	Length	Weigh	Length	Weigh
20	3.1	46	46	72	196.5
21	3.6	47	49.3	73	205.5
22	4.2	48	52.8	74	214.7
23	4.9	49	56.5	75	224.3
24	5.6	50	60.3	76	234.1
25	6.4	51	64.3	77	244.3
26	7.2	52	68.5	78	254.7
27	8.2	53	72.8	79	265.4
28	9.2	54	77.4	80	276.5
29	10.3	55	82.1	81	287.8
30	11.5	56	87	82	299.5
31	12.8	57	92.2	83	311.5
32	14.2	58	97.5	84	323.8
33	15.7	59	103.1	85	336.5
34	17.3	60	108.9	86	349.5
35	19	61	114.8	87	362.8
36	20.8	62	121.1	88	376.5
37	22.7	63	127.5	89	390.5
38	24.8	64	134.2	90	404.9
39	27	65	141.1	91	419.7
40	29.3	66	148.2	92	434.8
41	31.7	67	155.6	93	450.3
42	34.3	68	163.3	94	466.2
43	37	69	171.2	95	482.4
44	39.8	70	179.4	96	499.1
45	42.9	71	187.8		

8 PROCESSING THE CATCH

*T*he mantra concerning any fish destined for consumption is "Kill it, cool it, clean it." How and when this takes place usually depends on the size of the boat from which you are fishing. The 40-foot *Silver Fox* has a massive, refrigerated cooler built right on the fantail, while Ralph Shaw settles for several refreezable plastic ice containers in a small Coleman cooler aboard his 17-foot Boston Whaler Montauk. Many anglers, however, don't bother with ice at all, feeling that as long as fish are kept cool for the few hours before cleaning and filleting there won't be any problems, especially during cool weather conditions. I believe they are right. Fish stored for a few hours inside in-hull storage containers are still damp and cool to the touch when removed. During warm weather, however, especially if there is a hot sun, fish stored in the open should be fully covered. I have seen layers of kelp fronds, burlap sacks, and old terrycloth bath towels used with success, but they must be dampened periodically so that evaporation has a cooling effect.

Cleaning and Filleting

Members of the flatfish family seem to be designed for easy filleting, for you need only follow the "dotted lines" with a sharp knife to achieve success. The well-defined lateral line on each side (actually the back and belly) effectively separates the body into four quarters, so whether dealing with a 12-inch flounder or a 6-foot halibut, the basic steps are

(1) Make the first cut across the wrist of the tail as deep as the spine.

(2) Make the second cut along the lateral line toward the head, again cutting down to the spine.

(3) The third will be an angled cut behind the stomach cavity.

(4) Now turn the blade toward the tail and cut outward along the bones, rolling the fillet outward as it comes free.

(5) Next cut close behind the gill collar on the dorsal side.

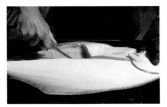

(6) Turn the blade toward the tail and cut outward along the bones.

(7) Roll the fillet outward as you work, then cut the skin to free it.

(8) Flip the fish over and make the first cut across the wrist of the tail as deep as the spine.

(9) Cut along the lateral line toward the head, cutting down to the spine.

(10) Cut close behind the gill collar on the dorsal side then make an angled cut behind the stomach cavity.

(11) Turn the blade toward the tail and cut outward along the bones, rolling the fillet outward as it comes free.

(12) Starting behind the gill collar on the dorsal side, turn the blade toward the tail and cut outward along the bones.

(13) Roll the fillet outward as you work and cut the skin to free the fillet.

(14) Feel around the cheek to determine its size and the position of the bones surrounding it then use the knife point to cut around the curved portion of the cheek bone. A bit of judicious carving will release the entire cheek muscle, which many consider the ultimate epicurean delight.

(15) Four beautiful fillets will now be ready for eating or further processing.

similar. The time and physical effort involved in handling larger fish obviously increases accordingly, but the end result provides just that much more outstanding food.

Your working surface should be flat, long enough and wide enough to support the fish and at a comfortable working height. A sharp filleting knife is a must, but keep your sharpening steel or Carborundum stone handy to touch up the cutting edge as required.

Unless you are filleting your fish at home, the skin must be left on the fillets for identification purposes. You may, however, cut each fillet into manageable sized pieces to package it for transportation. Consult a current copy of the *British Columbia Tidal Waters Sport Fishing Guide* for instructions concerning proper preparation, packaging and transportation of your catch.

Gutting

If you are keeping your halibut in the round with the head on, insert the knifepoint into the anus and cut forward up the belly to the throat. Cut around in front of the gill collar, and then cut the gill arches free at the top and bottom of the throat. Ensure that all of the gills are removed to prevent tainting the flesh.

After removing the guts from the body cavity, go to the top rear of the cavity and remove the gonads from each side of the spine. Female ovaries are pinkish, triangular-shaped hollow sacs, while male testes are

To remove worms:

A wise old commercial fisherman once told me, "If you don't like eating fish with worms in 'em, then don't look too hard for worms 'cause you can always find 'em." While I have since followed this advice with all species of fish, I still look for the obvious ones. In the case of halibut, they are small C-shaped grubs found in the lower belly flesh. I don't doubt for a heartbeat that I have probably eaten many of the little buggers over the years, but when processing my own fish, I always remove those I can find easily. Whether fresh or frozen and thawed, after skinning a piece of flesh from the belly area, you should hold it up to a strong light—even sunlight will work. If any grubs are present, they can be easily detected and removed by simply digging them out or trimming off the piece containing them. Jason Mohl, the owner/operator of Jay's Clayoquot Ventures at Tofino, spent some time working as a commercial fisherman before getting into the recreational field. He suggests that no matter how a fish is landed, once it is subdued or dead it should be laid on its back, belly up, for at least one hour before it is processed. For whatever reason, the nematode grubs that are usually present in the belly meat of most halibut will gather in the stomach cavity itself. This makes avoiding them while filleting just that much easier.

grey or light brown rubbery-looking tissue. Scrape out the kidney from alongside the spine, and then wash the body cavity and wipe it dry.

Chalkiness

On occasion you might encounter a fish with a condition called "chalky flesh." Rather than the normal translucent white, it is opaque white, almost as if it has already been cooked. This condition is the result of a build-up of lactic acid that occurs while a fish is struggling. It isn't usually apparent when a fish is being processed but instead develops over a period that may range from a couple of hours to several days. It is not a health hazard, and while the flesh has quite acceptable flavour, it is somewhat drier and best suited for deep-frying in batter.

Chalky halibut (right) is best suited for deep frying in batter.
(Courtesy of International Pacific Halibut Commission)

The Fine Art of Freezing Fish

Most people consider frozen fish inferior in quality and taste to freshly caught, and the truth is that this is often the case. However, frozen fish of questionable flavour were probably inferior when they went into the freezer. At best, freezing will maintain taste and quality; it cannot improve it.

But even if you have properly cared for your fish beforehand, freezer burn will result in fish flesh that has the taste and texture of rancid blotting paper. The cause is cold air drawing moisture out of the flesh until it becomes desiccated and stringy. Fortunately, there are methods to prevent air from reaching the flesh.

Wrapping Materials

The best wrapping materials to use are heavy-duty plastic "cling wraps" or aluminum foil. While wrapping the fish, ensure that all air has been squeezed from the package before sealing it. Then cover with heavy-duty freezer wrap to prevent punctures.

Glazing

The most efficient method for long-term storage is glazing the flesh with ice. Dip each piece in ice-cold water, then place it on a plate inside the freezer and leave it until a film of ice forms. (Vera uses metal cookie sheets for this stage.) Repeat this step until ice builds to about $\frac{1}{8}$- to $\frac{1}{4}$-inch thick. Cover with freezer wrap to prevent the ice from chipping.

Freezing in Ice

Freeze steaks or fillets in water-filled containers such as polyester freezer bags (not polyethylene), glass or plastic containers or waxed cardboard milk cartons. After totally immersing the fish in ice water, knead it down with a spatula to release all trapped air. After freezing, cover any exposed flesh with ice water and refreeze.

Machines that will shrink-wrap and heat-seal fish in plastic bags range in price from $40 to $400 and, yes, you get what you pay for. Thin-gauge plastic material is best for vacuum sealing, but you will need to use a heavier gauge if the bags are to be water-filled.

Home Freezing

To maintain top quality, fish must be frozen as soon as possible after catching and as quickly as possible once it is in the freezer. But while home freezers are great at keeping food frozen, they are terribly inefficient at initially freezing it. This is because in a typical home freezer the chilling process relies on refrigerant pumped through cooling coils. Warm air from the interior is absorbed by the refrigerant and carried outside where the heat dissipates. But your home freezer only operates at about -10° Celsius so it might take 24 hours to freeze a 10-pound package of fillets, whereas a large commercial freezer, which has a greater capacity and more refrigerant and cooling surface and operates at -35° Celsius, can freeze a ton of fish in two hours.

Opening a freezer lid or door warms the interior, and even after the lid is closed, the temperature will not drop back down until the refrigeration coils absorb and remove that warmed air. And whenever a package at room temperature is placed in a freezer, it generates more warmth, further slowing the process. Large packages—say 10 percent or more of a freezer's capacity—raise its temperature by up to 11° Celsius.

You can assist your home freezer by chilling your fish beforehand with a mixture of 20 parts crushed ice to one part pickling salt. Spread the ice three inches deep in a cooler that has an open drain at the bottom. Add a layer of fish or fillets that have been sealed in plastic wrap or aluminum foil. Fill the spaces between each package with crushed ice. Cover with more ice, then another layer of fish. Cover the last layer with about three inches of ice.

Once the lid has been tightly closed, the cooler's internal temperature will lower to -2° Celsius, quickly chilling the fish. This system is ideal for boats or campers as it will keep fish in excellent condition for up to one week. Upon arrival home, you can transfer the chilled fish into your freezer with minimal impact on its refrigeration system.

Alternately, if your refrigerator has a frost-free freezer compartment, transfer its contents into your home freezer, then use the compartment to freeze your fish. Once it is frozen, transfer it immediately to the freezer. Never store fish in a frost-free freezer compartment as it will dry out quickly.

The freezing efficiency of any freezer can also be increased by placing "heat sinks" in it. These are small containers filled with a eutectic solution—pickling salt and water—which does not freeze until it reaches -21° Celsius (water freezes at 0° Celsius).

All ingredients are by weight: pickling salt: 23 percent; water: 77 percent (11 ½ lb salt + 38 ½ lb water = 50 pounds).

Be warned that this solution is extremely corrosive, so plastic water containers are recommended. Freezing the tightly sealed containers takes up to a week, but this ice stays frozen much longer than regular ice before starting to melt. When packaged fish are placed in the freezer, these containers of ice quickly absorb their heat, which is then transferred gradually to the refrigeration system. And to speed the freezing process even more, place the frozen heat sinks and plastic-wrapped fish in a suitable-sized dishpan then cover with a chilled solution of the same salt brine. When steaks or fillets treated in this way are placed in the freezer, they will freeze solid in about one hour.

PART THREE

9 TRAVEL AND ACCOMMODATION GUIDE AND MARINE CHART COORDINATES

• •

*T*he coordinates listed in the Marine Chart section are intended only for reference and planning purposes. All were calculated by the authors and are believed to be correct, but none of them should ever be used for navigation purposes until validated by crosschecking on the specific marine chart indicated. You, as the user, must assume full responsibility for determining the accuracy of any coordinates listed. Prior to making any critical navigational decision you must consult official sources, including marine charts and the monthly "Notices to Mariners."

Most of the place names following each destination are taken from the *Gazetteer of Canada - British Columbia.* In cases where a name does not appear in the *Gazetteer* or is a local name, coordinates have been taken from the specific marine charts. Local names are shown within quotation marks to indicate that they are not shown on charts.

Read the latitudes northward from bottom to top of the chart and longitudes westward from right to left. Do not consider the coordinates as "hotspots" but rather as locations to help you get around specific areas in order to locate those hotspots. Programming a coordinate into your GPS beforehand will put you in "the ballpark," but the waypoint for a specific hotspot should always be programmed on site for best results in relocating it

The Southern Tip of Vancouver Island
SIDNEY, VICTORIA AND SOOKE

The key words when planning halibut trips—more or less in order—are "dependable fish abundance," "ease of accessibility," "reasonable weather conditions" and "travel distance to fishing areas." One area that does quite well in all four categories is the southern end of

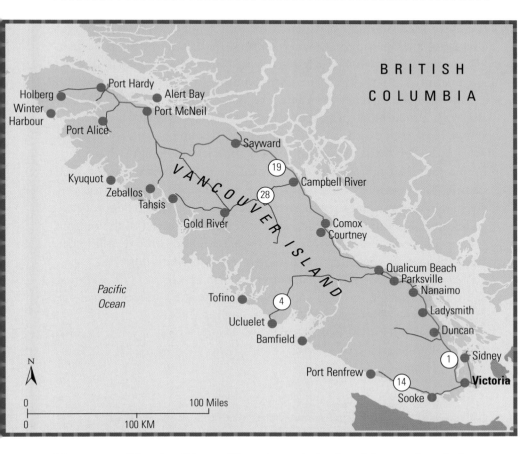

Vancouver Island—Sidney, Victoria and Sooke. I have placed them together here because local anglers from all three areas crisscross back and forth, depending on where the action is being reported, so the hotspots are interchangeable.

In addition to excellent resident and migratory chinook fishing, plus coho, pink, sockeye and chum salmon runs that vary in abundance from year to year, this entire area yields noteworthy catches of halibut every year—everything from 10-pound chickens to 200-pound-plus barn doors. In 2006, for example, 450 tickets were sold for the annual two-day "Just for the Halibut Derby" in Victoria, which is hosted by Island Outfitters, 100.3 "Q" Radio, and 1200 CKXM Country. Proceeds go to the "Q" TLC Kids Fund at the Queen Alexandra Foundation for Children. Held on April 22-23, this derby saw 102 halibut weighed in, 9 of them over 100 pounds. The winning fish—197.4 pounds—was caught by Don Vandijk, who also boated an 89.8-pounder the day before.

Despite these impressive catch records, anglers seldom encounter the dense crowds found elsewhere around the Island during peak fishing periods, probably because such a vast area offers so many fishing opportunities. It's 67 km by road from Sidney to Sooke via Victoria and about the same distance by water. The area's marine charts graphically illustrate the number of potential fishing spots—over 100 by name—inlets, bays, islands, shoals, reefs, pinnacles, rockpiles, and sharp drop-offs to deeper water. These all create the type of habitat that offers ample food and relative safety for creatures at the bottom of the food chain—herring, anchovies, sand lance (needlefish), shrimp, prawns, squid and crabs —and they in turn attract the fish that feed upon them. In addition to halibut, you can expect to encounter most of the bottom fish species common to the West Coast, including brown, quillback, tiger and widow rockfish, cabezon, kelp greenling and lingcod.

As the southern end of Vancouver Island is also popular with the sailing and boating set, there are several marinas in the area. However, launch ramps are located only at the following:

Saanich Inlet: Mill Bay Marina, 740 Handy Road; Tsartlip Launch Ramp, 800 Stellys Cross Road; Goldstream Boathouse, 2892 Trans Canada Highway.

Don Vandijk (left) with his 197.4-pound "Just for the Halibut Derby" winner with Island Outfitters owners Darren Wright and Ward Bond.

Sidney: Island View Beach at the end of Island View Road; VanIsle Marina, 2320 Harbour Road; Roberts Bay Public Launch, Ardwell Road (cartoppers only); Sidney Public Launch Ramp (Tulista Park), McTavish Road off Lochside Drive.

Victoria: James Bay Anglers' Association, 75 Dallas Road; The Marina at Oak Bay, 1327 Beach Drive; Pedder Bay Marina, 925 Pedder Bay Drive.

Becher Bay: Cheanuh Marina, 4901 East Sooke Road; Pacific Lions Marina, 241 Becher Bay Road.

Sooke: Sunny Shores Marina, 5621 Sooke Road; Jock's Dock and Crab Shack, 6947 West Coast Road.

Weather and Water Conditions

Southern Vancouver Island enjoys a moderate climate with heavy rainfall confined mostly to the relatively mild winter months. Summers are generally dry and pleasant.

Fog is not as consistent as farther north, but it can occur whenever the conditions are right between August and mid-autumn. As fog can form very quickly, get off the water at the first sign of it unless your boat is equipped with a compass and GPS.

Northeasters and southeasters are the prevailing winter winds, with northeasters usually the worst. Summer winds are generally westerlies or southwesters; a southeaster usually means bad weather conditions. While there might be no winds to speak of on some summer days and most areas remain fairly calm during the mornings, more often than not thermal winds can be expected anywhere from noon to 2 p.m., easing off toward 6 p.m. Depending on the tides, you can plan on a morning and evening fishery, but tide changes mixed with brisk winds can make for conditions that are best avoided.

Although halibut are present all year, unless the weather is agree-

Sooke is a popular fishing area as well as a good departure point for the offshore banks.

able, the fishery doesn't usually start getting serious until April. True, some diehards start as soon after the February 1 opening as possible and they continue chasing them until the next January 1 closure, but these anglers are relatively few in number. September generally offers relatively calm water conditions, making it a pleasant time for halibut fishing until the autumn rains and winds arrive, usually at some point during October.

Popular halibut haunts in the Sidney area include Sidney Channel as far south as D'Arcy Shoals, between James Island and Cordova Spit, Cordova Channel (right off Cordova Spit), and Miners Channel around Mandarte Island and Halibut Island. Generally, any area with a flat, sandy or gravel bottom offers good potential.

A 48-metre shelf southeast of Rudlin Bay, located on the south side of Discovery Island, is

Larry Stefanyk hooked this halibut off Sooke while fishing with a spreader bar, dink sinker and salmon belly.

worth checking out, as is the bait-rich area around the Chain Islets between Discovery Island and Oak Bay. Brodie Rock, just off Gonzales Point, also has the sort of underwater structure that attracts bait, as do the Trial Islands and Brotchie Ledge off Ogden Point.

Victoria anglers can head out from Pedder Bay and be in halibut water at the 11 fathom marker located just off the mouth. Race Passage and Race Rocks—which yield some of the best halibut catches in the entire area—are nearby, Constance Bank is just a short run northeast, and Border (Coyote) Bank a short jog southward toward the Olympic Peninsula. If there is nothing doing at these popular hotspots, anglers can simply sneak around the corner and head west to try a few Sooke area hotspots like Secretary (Donaldson) Island and Otter Point, right on up to Point No Point. The latter area lends itself well to downrigging close to the bottom, which permits covering a lot of territory and has the added bonus of also attracting some fair-sized feeder chinooks.

Most anglers who intentionally target halibut use salmon bellies or large herring drifted along the bottom with spreader bars and sinkers weighing up to two pounds, but some go after them with drift jigs, top-rigged jigs and leadheads, usually sweetened with fresh bait or scent for added attraction.

Whatever your choice, fish during small tide changes and the slack periods in between, which provide better chances of getting your bait or lure down deep and keeping it there. If you plan on downrigging, study the applicable marine chart before dropping the cannonballs. There are several areas where the bottom rises sharply and these can prove expensive.

Once your gear is down, monitor your depth sounder closely to avoid hang-ups. Stay aware of how the tidal currents are affecting your trolling patterns. Water flowing between and around the islands, shoals and reefs gets quite swift in some areas, and a boat that appears to be going straight ahead might actually be pushed sideways into shallow water.

Guide's Tip:

Halibut don't always feed right on the bottom, so if the bites are slow or non-existent try about 15 to 20 feet up from the bottom.

Keep your hooks sticky sharp. A halibut can suck in food in a microsecond and spit it out just as fast. That needle-sharp point improves your chances of hooking it.

When I'm drifting for halibut, the very moment that a rod starts to move I hit the GPS and mark the spot before I grab the rod. If it's a halibut, I keep the mark, if not I erase it.

Marine Chart Coordinates:

Place Names:		Place Names:	
Aldridge Point	LAT48°46' LONG 123°15'	Mouat Point	LAT 48°47' LONG 123°19'
Alldridge Point	LAT 48°19' LONG 123°38'	North Pender Island	LAT 48°47' LONG 123°17'
Arbutus Island	LAT 48°42' LONG 123°26'	O'Brien Point	LAT 48°20' LONG 123°42'
Becher Bay	LAT 48°20' LONG 123°37'	Oak Bay	LAT 48°26' LONG 123°18
Bedford Islands	LAT 48°19' LONG 123°36'	Ogden Point	LAT 48°25' LONG 123°23'
Bedwell Harbour	LAT 48°45' LONG 123°15'	Otter Point	LAT 48°21' LONG 123°49'
Beechey Head	LAT 48°19' LONG 123°39'	Pedder Bay	LAT 48°20' LONG 123°33'
Bentinck Island	LAT 48°19' LONG 123°32'	Piers Island	LAT 48°42' LONG 123°25'
"Border (Coyote) Bank"	LAT 48°18' LONG 123°17'	Point Fairfax	LAT 48°42' LONG 123°16'
Brethour Island	LAT 48°41' LONG 123°19'	Point No Point	LAT 48°23' LONG 123°59'
Brodie Rock	LAT 48°24' LONG 123°17'	Possession Point	LAT 48°20' LONG 123°43'
Brotchie Ledge	LAT 48°24' LONG 123°23'	"Powder Wharf"	LAT 48°36' LONG 123°20'
Cape Keppel	LAT 48°43' LONG 123°29'	Prevost Passage	LAT 48°42' LONG 123°19'
Cattle Point	LAT 48°27' LONG 123°17'	Pym Island	LAT 48°42' LONG 123°23'
Charmer Point	LAT 48°41' LONG 123°21'	Race Passage	LAT 48°18' LONG 123°32'
Cherry Point	LAT 48°43' LONG 123°33'	Race Rocks	LAT 48°18' LONG 123°32'
Chatham Island	LAT 48°26' LONG 123°15'	"Red Can Buoy"	LAT 48°38' LONG 123°21'
Christopher Point	LAT 48°19' LONG 123°34	Saanich Peninsula	LAT 48°37' LONG 123°26'
Church Island	LAT 48°19' LONG 123°35'	Saanich Inlet	LAT 48°37' LONG 123°30'
Clover Point	LAT 48°24' LONG 123°21'	Sansum Narrows	LAT 48°48' LONG 123°34'
Coal Island	LAT 48°41' LONG 123°22'	Saseenos	LAT 48°23' LONG 123°40'
Cod Reefs (North and South)	LAT 48°40' LONG 123°18'	Satellite Channel	LAT 48°43' LONG 123°26'
Colburne Passage	LAT 48°42' LONG 123°25'	Saxe Point	LAT 48°25' LONG 123°25'
Constance Bank	LAT 48°21' LONG 123°21'	Separation Point	LAT 48°44' LONG 123°34
Cordova Channel	LAT 50°26' LONG 125°35'	Seymour Point	LAT 48°43' LONG 123°20'
Cordova (Saanichton) Spit	LAT 48°36' LONG 123°22'	Shag Rock	LAT 48°41' LONG 123°23'
D'Arcy Island	LAT 48°34' LONG 123°17'	Sheringham Point	LAT 48°23' LONG 123°55'
D'Arcy Shoals	LAT 48°34' LONG 123°18'	Shute Passage	LAT 48°43' LONG 123°23'
Discovery Island	LAT 48°25' LONG 123°14'	Shute Reef	LAT 48°43' LONG 123°26'
Dock Island	LAT 48°40' LONG 123°21'	Sidney Channel	LAT 48°37' LONG 123°20'
Domville Island	LAT 48°40' LONG 123°19'	Sidney Island	LAT 48°37' LONG 123°20'
Donaldson (Secretary) Island	LAT 48°20' LONG 123°42'	Sidney Spit	LAT 48°39' LONG 123°20'
East Sooke	LAT 48°22' LONG 123°41	Sidney	LAT 48°39' LONG 123°24'
Forrest Island	LAT 48°40' LONG 123°20'	Sooke	LAT 48°23' LONG 123°43'
Frazer Island	LAT 48°20' LONG 123°37'	Sooke Basin	LAT 48°23' LONG 123°40'
"Gap, The"	LAT 48°26' LONG 123°14'	Sooke Harbour	LAT 48°22' LONG 123°43'
Gonzales Point ("Golf Links")	LAT 48°24' LONG 123°18'	Sooke Inlet	LAT 48°21' LONG 123°43'
Gordons Beach	LAT 48°22' LONG 123°50'	Sooke Bluffs	LAT 48°21' LONG 123°45'
Halibut Island	LAT 48°37' LONG 123°16'	South Pender Island	LAT 48°45' LONG 123°13'
Haro Strait	LAT 48°35' LONG 123°19'	Swanson Channel	LAT 48°46' LONG 123°19'
Hatch Point	LAT 48°42' LONG 123°32'	Swartz Bay	LAT 48°41' LONG 123°24'
Holland Point	LAT 48°25' LONG 123°22'	Swiftsure Bank	LAT 48°33' LONG 125°00'
Imrie Island	LAT 48°42' LONG 123°20'	Ten Mile Point	LAT 48°27' LONG 123°16'
James Island	LAT 48°36' LONG 123°21'	"Trap Shack"	LAT 48°19' LONG 123°41'
Killer Whale Point	LAT 48°41' LONG 123°23'	Trial Islands	LAT 48°24' LONG 123°18'
Knapp Island	LAT 48°42' LONG 123°24'	Tulista Park	LAT 48°38' LONG 123°24'
Macaulay Point	LAT 48°25' LONG 123°25'	Victoria Harbour	LAT 48°25' LONG 123°24'
Mandarte Island	LAT 48°38' LONG 123°17'	Village Spit	LAT 48°37' LONG 123°23'
Miners Channel	LAT 48°38' LONG 123°17'	Wain Rock	LAT 48°41' LONG 123°29'
Moresby Island	LAT 48°43' LONG 123°19'	Whiffen Spit	LAT 48°21' LONG 123°45'
Moses Point	LAT 48°41' LONG 123°29'	Whirl Bay	LAT 48°19' LONG 123°35'

Available Marine Charts:

3310 Gulf Islands - Victoria Harbour to Nanaimo Harbour
3440 Race Rocks to D'Arcy Island
3441 Haro Strait, Boundary Pass and Satellite Channel
3461 Juan de Fuca Strait, Eastern Portion
3462 Juan de Fuca Strait to Strait of Georgia
3476 Approaches to Tsehum Harbour
3641 Albert Head to Otter Point

East Coast Destinations
PORT HARDY

Northern Vancouver Island's largest community (about 3,800 residents) has a full range of accommodations: fishing lodges, motels, hotels, bed-and-breakfast operations and serviced campgrounds. However, accommodations are scarce during the summer months when BC Ferries increases sailings between Port Hardy and Prince Rupert. In addition, from July through September their Discovery Coast Passage ferry docks on alternate nights to the Prince Rupert ferry. Since ferry passengers reserve overnight stays in Port Hardy well in advance, finding a room on short notice ranges from difficult to impossible. Trust me, for I write this based on experience: if you are planning a summer fishing trip out of Port Hardy, book well in advance.

Port Hardy is a popular summer destination so it is wise to book accommodation and moorage well in advance.

Port Hardy area waters are dotted with islands that provide excellent habitat for all fish species.

Visitors may fly to Port Hardy via Pacific Coastal Airlines, which offers scheduled flights from Vancouver. By road, Port Hardy is approximately 530 km from Sidney, 500 km from Victoria, 390 km from Nanaimo, and 280 km from the Comox international airport, which is serviced from out-of-province by WestJet and Air Canada.

The Glen Lyon Inn is noted for its early morning breakfasts, I.V.'s Quarterdeck Pub for its hearty pub grub and the Airport Inn for excellent Chinese food. The area also boasts Hardy Buoys Smoked Fish, a large, modern operation where anglers can have their catch processed and prepared for shipment and where they can purchase everything from live crabs to fresh fish to smoked salmon. Be warned that their Indian Candy smoked chum salmon is truly addictive.

If you are using your own boat, be aware that the government wharf is usually plugged with commercial fishing vessels throughout the summer. Moorage is available at Quarterdeck Marina on a daily, weekly or monthly basis, but book well in advance.

There is a free municipal launch ramp at Quarterdeck Marina. It is concrete and three lanes wide, but watch the drop-off on extremely low tides. Pay parking is available at the marina office, and there is limited free parking about two blocks from the ramp. Another free launch ramp is located at Bear Cove, near the BC Ferry terminal. This asphalt ramp has a fairly sharp drop-off, making it an excellent place to launch small

The free launch at Bear Cove near the BC Ferry terminal in Hardy Bay.

boats and cartoppers. There is ample free parking.

Hardy Bay Boat Rental offers 16 ½- to 19-foot boats. There are several independent fishing guides in the area, and the Port Hardy Charter Boat Association includes a number of experienced guides with Coast Guard inspected cabin cruisers ranging from 20 to 40 feet.

Weather and Water Conditions

Port Hardy enjoys a fairly moderate climate, but as rainfall averages 250-300 cm a year, appropriate wet weather clothing is a must.

Mariners consider the waters of Queen Charlotte Strait some of the most treacherous on the BC coast. Winter southeasters, prevalent from mid-October until May, may blow for two weeks straight without dropping below 50 kmh. Although summer northwest-

For visitor information:

PORT HARDY VISITOR CENTRE
7250 Market Street
Box 249
Port Hardy, BC, V0N 2P0
(250) 949-7622
phcc@cablerocket.com
www.ph-chamber.bc.ca

ers are generally considered safe, they can turn dangerous. While they are often gentle on dull, overcast days, they can build quickly to 80 kmh on clear, sunny days, creating waves to 6 feet high or more. Thus, even on nice days with calm water, you should watch the horizon for dark wind lines and monitor your radio for possible weather changes.

April southeasters might reduce fishing opportunities, but the May through June period usually offers pleasant weather conditions. July and August can also be good, but expect fog. Aside from occasional rain or windy conditions, September through mid- to late October is generally fair to good; after that, the serious winter weather sets in.

Many anglers use 14-foot boats with 20- to 30-hp outboards in Hardy Bay, but something more substantial is recommended for fishing much beyond the Bay. Offshore boats should be seaworthy and carry the minimum of a compass and VHF radio. Fog during late summer is

Tremble Island, near the mouth of Seymour Inlet, is located across the Inside Passage from Port Hardy.

common, so a GPS can be beneficial, and radar makes moving around even safer.

A marine chart of Queen Charlotte Strait reveals its potential for bottom fish. Multitudes of islands, rock piles, shoals, pinnacles, deep pockets and steep drop-offs provide a wealth of opportunities. There are some interesting possibilities right in Hardy Bay and around Duval Point, Daphne Point and the Masterman Islands.

Halibut are present here all year, but being migratory they can be difficult to locate at times. They are available right after the January closure and their numbers usually start increasing shortly after Easter, though June through September is generally their most active period. A few are still around in October, but most migrate elsewhere and do so surprisingly fast. They average 20 to 50 pounds, though several of 100-plus pounds are weighed in each season, and a few usually exceed 200 pounds.

Most halibut are taken offshore in 200 to 400 feet of water over areas with a fairly flat bottom. Popular spots are Bolivar Passage, Ripple Passage, Richards Channel, along the eastern drop-offs of the various island groups and offshore around Taylor Bank and Morgan Shoal. Anglers with fast boats may range east as far as the Numas Islands or west to Farquhar Bank. A depth sounder is a must for locating these hotspots and a GPS will make it even easier.

Heavy top-rigged jigs and drift jigs are popular here, as are spreader bars with fresh baits, Berkley Power Grubs or other soft plastic action baits. The same deep-water tactics, lures and baits will also attract yelloweye rockfish and lingcod, especially in areas with pinnacles, rocky bottoms and drop-offs. Check with the local tackle shops to find out which skirt colours and soft plastic lures are working best.

Available Marine Charts:

3547 Queen Charlotte Strait, Eastern Portion (Stuart Narrows, Kenneth Passage)

3548 Queen Charlotte Strait, Central Portion (Blunden Harbour, Port Hardy

3551 Jeannette Islands to Cape Caution

3574 Numas Island to Harris Island

3575 Goletas Channel to Pine Island (Bull Harbour)

3597 Pulteney Point to Egg Island

Guide's Tip:

Large shoals or flats will generally hold chickens, whereas structure attracts larger fish. A big part of a large halibut's diet is rockfish, which usually congregate around the base of reefs and rock piles.

When drifting over structure, fishing "downhill" will help you find the base of drop-offs where baitfish tend to congregate when the tide starts running.

A typical setup for halibut fishing in the Port Hardy area is a dink jig with a glow hoochie. Tipping the hook with a chunk of octopus provides some extra, long-lasting attraction.

Really pound the bottom with your jig. The scent and sight of a lure attracts halibut, but so does sound. This is important when fishing in an area with little tide movement or where the fish are scattered. The pounding can be heard over a long distance, so the fish will usually approach to check it out even if the jig can't initially be seen or smelled.

Marine Chart Coordinates:

Place Names:		Place Names:	
Balaklava Island	LAT 50°51' LONG 127°37'	Gordon Islands	LAT 50°49' LONG 127°28'
Bear Cove	LAT 50°43' LONG 127°28'	Hardy Bay	LAT 50°44' LONG 127°28'
Beaver Harbour	LAT 50°42' LONG 127°24'	Heard Island	LAT 50°50' LONG 127°31'
Bell Island	LAT 50°50' LONG 127°32'	Hurst Island	LAT 50°50' LONG 127°35'
Bolivar Passage	LAT 50°54' LONG 127°33'	Hussar Point	LAT 50°51' LONG 127°39'
Boxer Point	LAT 50°50' LONG 127°39'	Jeannette Islands	LAT 50°55' LONG 127°25'
Browning Islands	LAT 50°54' LONG 127°20'	Masterman Islands	LAT 50°45' LONG 127°25'
Cattle Island	LAT 50°43' LONG 127°24'	Millar Group	LAT 50°55' LONG 127°26'
Deer Island	LAT 50°43' LONG 127°23'	Morgan Shoal	LAT 50°47' LONG 127°15'
Deserters Group	LAT 50°53' LONG 127°29'	Nigei Island	LAT 50°53' LONG 127°45'
Dillon Point	LAT 50°54' LONG 127°24'	Peel Island	LAT 50°44' LONG 127°24'
Duncan Island	LAT 50°49' LONG 127°33'	Raynor Group	LAT 50°53' LONG 127°14'
Duval Island	LAT 50°46' LONG 127°30'	Richards Channel	LAT 50°57' LONG 127°27'
Duval Point	LAT 50°46' LONG 127°29'	Ripple Passage	LAT 50°54' LONG 127°27'
Frankham Point	LAT 50°47' LONG 127°35'	Round Island	LAT 50°43' LONG 127°22'
Goletas Channel	LAT 50°49' LONG 127°44'	Taylor Bank	LAT 50°50' LONG 127°16'
Gordon Channel	LAT 50°52' LONG 127°35'	Walker Group	LAT 50°54' LONG 127°32'

PORT MCNEILL AND TELEGRAPH COVE

Lower Queen Charlotte Strait and Blackfish Sound offer excellent bottom fishing prospects. Serious halibut fishing starts in April and continues through June. Most fish weigh 20 to 30 pounds, but they do get much larger. A few big fish are usually caught during July, but fishing slows down somewhat in August and early September then picks up again in late September.

Between Port McNeill and Telegraph Cove, visiting anglers have a wide range of accommodations from which to choose. Both communities provide quick access to popular fishing areas and in the event of inclement weather have the added attraction of offering fair to good fishing in protected waters bordering the shoreline.

Road access to Telegraph Cove is off Highway 19 at a well-marked turnoff about 7 km southeast of Port McNeill. The first turnoff to the left off the access road leads to Alder Bay Resort, offering 88 sites, a convenience store, a two-lane concrete launch ramp, moorage and other amenities.

After the pavement ends, the gravel road continues past the Canadian Forest Products dryland sorting and booming grounds at Beaver Cove. The next marked turn-off to the left leads 2.6 km to Hidden Cove Lodge, which has 8 rooms in the main lodge and 2 roomy

Many good halibut haunts can be found in the Port McNeill area bordering Blackfish Sound.

cabins. Located in a secluded cove, this operation is noted for comfortable accommodations, good service and outstanding meals.

About 12 km from the highway, the main road ends at Telegraph Cove where you will find a convenience store, restaurant, concrete launch ramp, 135-berth marina, boat rentals and cabins. The only fuel dock in the immediate area is located at the end of the boardwalk.

Alder Bay and Telegraph Cove are launching spots for several remote fishing resorts located on islands in the Blackfish Sound area. These lodges are also accessible by chartered floatplanes from Vancouver, Campbell River or Port Hardy, the latter two destinations being served daily by scheduled flights from Vancouver.

Weather and Water Conditions

Take warm clothing and rain gear. During the summer months Blackfish Sound is fairly protected from Queen Charlotte Strait northeasters but afternoon westerlies are common. If they blow against the tide, the water can get rough. Depending on location, it's usually

For visitor information:

PORT MCNEILL VISITOR CENTRE
PO Box 129
Port McNeill, BC, V0N 2R0
(250) 956-3131
pmccc@island.net
www.portmcneill.net

possible to tuck into a bay
or the lee of an island
until water conditions
level out after the tide
change. Double Bay is a
good sanctuary or one
can duck through the
"Blow Hole" between
Hanson Island and the
Plumper Islands and usu-
ally find protected waters.

Halibut anglers should always have a few large green
hoochies in their tackle collections.

During tide changes, however, use caution at the "Blow Hole." Rapids
and whirlpools often form, and there are lots of barely submerged
rocks.

Blackney Passage also gets rough from Licka Point to Cracroft Point
on West Cracroft Island. This is a major thoroughfare for huge cruise
ships, freighters and log carriers, so whenever a large vessel
approaches—especially one running with the tide—get out of its way
as quickly as possible and then watch for the high following waves
resulting from its passage.

Fog is seldom a problem during the spring and early summer, but
from mid-August on, it can be. Having suitable navigation equipment
on board is a must as is knowing how to use it properly.

One of the most popular hotspots is Stubbs Island, halfway between
Malcolm and Hanson islands, but as it is surrounded by shoals, it can
be tough on tackle, especially off the north and east sides. Depending
on weather and water conditions, anglers also look for halibut from
Lizard Point on the northern side of Malcolm Island virtually right on
down through Blackney Passage to the Sophia Islands. As halibut are
migratory, today's hotspot might be dead tomorrow, so it pays to
prospect.

It was at Cracroft Point in 1993 that Lynn Gerig of Lebanon,
Oregon, used the remains of a filleted rockfish on a spreader bar to
attract a 259-pound halibut. Local anglers had avoided the Point
because of its rocky bottom, but fortunately for Gerig he was new to the
area and didn't know that.

Available Marine Charts:

3546 Broughton Strait

Marine Chart Coordinates:

Place Names:		Place Names:	
Alder Bay Campsite	LAT 50°34' LONG 126°55'	Licka Point	LAT 50°34' LONG 126°41'
Baronet Passage	LAT 50°33' LONG 126°35'	Lizard Point	LAT 50°40' LONG 126°53'
Bauza Cove Campground-Marina	LAT 50°33' LONG 126°49'	Malcolm Island	LAT 50°39' LONG 126°59'
Bell Rocks	LAT 50°33' LONG 126°39'	Mitchell Bay	LAT 50°38' LONG 126°51'
Blackfish Sound	LAT 50°35' LONG 126°43'	Neill Rock	LAT 50°36' LONG 127°03'
Blackney Passage	LAT 50°34' LONG 126°41'	Nowell Bank	LAT 50°45' LONG 126°51'
Blinkhorn Peninsula	LAT 50°33' LONG 126°47'	Numas Islands	LAT 50°46' LONG 126°06'
"Blow Hole"	LAT 50°35' LONG 126°47'	Parson Bay	LAT 50°34' LONG 126°39'
Bold Head	LAT 50°37' LONG 126°44'	Parson Island	LAT 50°34' LONG 126°40'
Broughton Island	LAT 50°49' LONG 126°45'	Pearse Islands	LAT 50°35' LONG 126°52'
Cormorant Channel	LAT 50°36' LONG 126°54'	Pearse Passage	LAT 50°35' LONG 126°53
Cracroft Point	LAT 50°33' LONG 126°40'	Plumper Islands	LAT 50°35' LONG 126°47'
Donegal Head	LAT 50°38' LONG 126°49'	Port McNeill	LAT 50°35' LONG 127°06'
Double Bay	LAT 50°35' LONG 126°46'	Pulteney Point	LAT 50°38' LONG 127°09'
Egeria Shoal	LAT 50°38' LONG 126°46'	Queen Charlotte Sound	LAT 51°30' LONG 128°30'
Ella Point	LAT 50°33' LONG 126°49'	Red Point	LAT 50°35' LONG 126°40'
Foster Island	LAT 50°42' LONG 126°50'	Sophia Islands	LAT 50°32' LONG 126°38'
Freshwater Bay	LAT 50°36' LONG 126°42'	Spout Islet	LAT 50°35' LONG 126°45'
George Bank	LAT 50°44' LONG 126°58'	Stubbs Island	LAT 50°36' LONG 126°49'
Haddington Passage	LAT 50°36' LONG 126°00'	Swanson Island	LAT 50°37' LONG 126°42'
Hanson Island	LAT 50°34' LONG 126°44'	Telegraph Cove	LAT 50°28' LONG 126°17'
Harbledown Island	LAT 50°34' LONG 126°35'	Trinity Bay	LAT 50°39' LONG 126°55'
Hidden Cove	LAT 50°33' LONG 126°51'	Wastell Islets	LAT 50°33' LONG 126°49'
Holford Islets	LAT 50°44' LONG 126°48'	Wedge Island	LAT 50°38' LONG 126°43'
Johnstone Strait	LAT 50°27' LONG 126°00'	West Cracroft Island	LAT 50°33' LONG 126°23'
Kenneth Bay	LAT 50°50' LONG 126°00'	West Passage	LAT 50°36' LONG 126°41'
Knight Inlet	LAT 50°47' LONG 126°38'	Weynton Passage	LAT 50°35' LONG 126°49'
Ledge Rock	LAT 50°41' LONG 126°41'	Whitebeach Passage	LAT 50°35' LONG 126°40'
Leonard Rock	LAT 50°36' LONG 126°58'		

SAYWARD

While Sayward offers most amenities and services, they are somewhat spread out. The White River Court, just west of Sayward Junction, has cabins, an RV park and cafe. Other accommodations in the area include Fisherboy Park with cabins, an RV park and a convenience store, the Salmon River Inn and Restaurant right in town, Kelsey Bay RV Park, Mount H'Kusam View Lodge, Victoria Garden Gate Manor, and the Salmon River Motel and Campgrounds. Other eateries are Charlie's Place and the Coral Reef Pub at the junction, and the Cable Cookhouse Cafe.

Until 1979 the Island Highway ended at Sayward, and the terminus

The island-studded waters of Johnstone Strait provide plenty of halibut habitat in the Sayward area, but there is a lot of rugged, tackle-grabbing bottom.

for the Prince Rupert ferry was located at Kelsey Bay at the northwestern corner of Salmon Bay. But after completion of the Highway 19 extension to Port Hardy, the highway was diverted 10 km south of Sayward, and the terminus was relocated at Bear Cove in Hardy Bay. Basically all that now remains in Sayward is the large terminus parking lot overlooking the Kelsey Bay Small Craft Harbour. The concrete, all-tide launch ramp here is suitable for large boats, and the launching and parking fee is reasonable. The small craft harbour offers daily and monthly moorage, and marine fuel is available.

For visitor information:

WHITE RIVER COURT
INFORMATION CENTRE
RR 1
Sayward, BC, V0P 1R0
(250) 282-3265

Just beyond the small craft harbour is the government wharf. To its left is an RV park with five sites and the Sayward Fish & Game Club launch ramp. This narrow, curving stretch of concrete is a real challenge to those unskilled at backing up with a boat trailer. Parking is quite limited.

A launch ramp that is located at the end of the old MacBlo causeway is the one most often used by local anglers. To get there you must drive onto the causeway, veer right at the dryland sort and follow the road around its perimeter. The roadway is well marked with signs. The ramp is steep and rocky, but there is plenty of parking.

Weather and Water Conditions

The valley in which Sayward lies enjoys fairly mild, drier weather than areas to the north and south, but suitable rain gear and warm clothing are always recommended. Fog becomes a possibility from mid-August on through fall.

A map of Vancouver Island shows Johnstone Strait stretching for 65 km from Telegraph Cove to the western tip of Hardwicke Island in a 4-km wide, fairly straight channel. At Hardwicke Point it deflects northeast up Sunderland Channel, but it continues past the mouth of Salmon Bay before it splits around Helmcken Island into Current and Race passages. But while this Strait often appears benign, it is definitely not small boat water. Tidal flows in Race Passage reach 11 kmh, creating tide rips that are best avoided. Southerly winds seldom cause problems, but even moderate westerlies are another story, especially when blowing against a running tide. However, if there is a westerly wind, it usually occurs during the middle of the day while mornings and evenings are often calm.

According to local fishing guide Hans Schuer, if the wind comes from the northeast, Hardwicke Island provides shelter. If it comes from the south, boats are sheltered by Vancouver Island and from the east by West Thurlow Island. "On anything but a west wind we are sheltered," Schuer explained, "so it's always fishable. But the west and northwest winds are bad—even a 5 km west wind builds up waves all the way along. We have bad rip tides here and with a west wind they can be really bad. I use my tide guide to see the difference between high and low then I stay away from the spots I know are bad. There is always a bad rip on the corner of Helmcken, so I simply stay away from it."

When fishing out of Sayward, don't let the calm-looking waters of Johnstone Strait fool you; some areas are best avoided in all but very seaworthy boats.

Guide's Tip:

Halibut or lingcod skin usually works
well as bait. It's very durable and lasts
through multiple bites.

Whenever a good bite comes on, note the
tidal conditions. Halibut will bite time
after time during the same stage of a tide.
I find this is a fairly accurate gauge for
up to a week or so, then things start
changing when the tides build up or slow
down.

Johnstone Strait is also a major thoroughfare for huge cruise ships, freighters and log carriers, and when they are running with the tide, high waves result from their passage. While a 14-foot boat is suitable when conditions are favourable, a 16-footer or larger makes much more sense.

However, the rugged, uneven bottom throughout this area is a halibut fisherman's (and lure manufacturer's) delight, yielding fish to 100 pounds or more. There are also fair-sized lingcod, plenty of greenling, and a good cross-section of the rockfish family.

A favoured hotspot is a huge shoal on the south side of Johnstone Strait, directly across from Blenkinsop Bay. Known locally as "The Shoal," it rises about 800 feet from the bottom to within 200 feet of the surface. Other halibut haunts are the mouth of Chancellor Channel off Eden Point, up into Wellbore Channel around Bulkely Island and at the top end of the Strait around the Midgham Islets and Althorp Point.

There are always a few halibut around in Johnstone Strait, but the best times are June and July, then September and October.

Available Marine Charts:

3544 Johnstone Strait (Race Passage and Current Passage)

Marine Chart Coordinates:

Place Names:		Place Names:	
Althorp Point	LAT 50°28' LONG 125°48'	Hkusam Bay	LAT 50°23' LONG 125°55'
Artillery Islets	LAT 50°26' LONG 125°59'	Johnstone Strait	LAT 50°26' LONG 126°00'
Blenkinsop Bay	LAT 50°29' LONG 126°00'	Kelsey Bay	LAT 50°24' LONG 125°58'
Brasseau Bay	LAT 50°24' LONG 125°58'	Midgham Islets	LAT 50°28' LONG 125°46'
Bulkely Island	LAT 50°26' LONG 125°44'	Race Passage	LAT 50°23' LONG 125°52'
Chancellor Channel	LAT 50°25' LONG 125°42'	Ripple Shoal	LAT 50°23' LONG 125°49'
Clarence Island	LAT 50°27' LONG 125°59'	Salmon Bay	LAT 50°23' LONG 125°57'
Current Passage	LAT 50°25' LONG 125°53'	Sayward	LAT 50°23' LONG 125°58'
Earl Ledge	LAT 50°25' LONG 125°55'	Sunderland Channel	LAT 50°28' LONG 125°53'
Eden Point	LAT 50°24' LONG 125°47'	"The Shoal"	LAT 50°27' LONG 126°02'
Fanny Island	LAT 50°27' LONG 125°59'	Tyee Point	LAT 50°23' LONG 125°47'
Graveyard Point	LAT 50°23' LONG 125°56'	Wellbore Channel	LAT 50°27' LONG 125°45'
Hardwicke Island	LAT 50°26' LONG 125°51'	West Thurlow Island	LAT 50°25' LONG 125°38'
Hardwicke Point	LAT 50°26' LONG 125°59'	Yorke Island	LAT 50°27' LONG 125°59'
Helmcken Island	LAT 50°24' LONG 125°52'		

Strait of Georgia Destinations

The history of halibut stocks in the Strait of Georgia remains somewhat of a mystery. Although they were certainly present prior to the introduction of commercial fishing, as no records were kept until the early 1900s, their original abundance is unknown. Studies indicate that a fairly substantial population was fished heavily for the Vancouver market, but whether those fish were year-round residents or migratory is anyone's guess. All of the studies make mention of Halibut Bank and it is reasonable to assume that it was named by commercial fishermen.

From the commercial fishing point of view the Strait of Georgia is now a non-starter, but recreational anglers should take note that the numbers being caught incidentally continue to increase, especially by those who are downrigging deep and close to the bottom for chinook salmon. Drift-jigging, which is also popular for deep-swimming chinooks, also attracts a fair number of the halibut that appear at the docks as incidental catches. Areas that have produced increasing numbers of halibut in recent years are Campbell River, the Comox Valley and the Nanoose Bay area between Parksville and Nanaimo. Most have been chickens in the 15- to 40-pound range but a few have topped 100 pounds.

The Strait of Georgia is a massive body of water that offers a multitude of potential halibut areas, but if there are any dedicated anglers currently fishing for them, their numbers are small—and they are not broadcasting the fact. That the fish are there is indisputable, but their population density continues to be followed by a big question mark. However, various marine charts will reveal hundreds of potential locations where they might be found, and based on what has been evolving over the past 10 years or so, all indications are that those who put in the time and effort to locate them might be pleasantly surprised at the results.

Lacking any useful halibut fishing information, I have lumped together most destinations in the Southern Strait of Georgia to provide readers with data concerning accommodations, launching ramps, marinas and so forth.

CAMPBELL RIVER

Although Campbell River is promoted as the "Salmon Capital of the World," since the popularity of downriggers has steadily shouldered motor mooching aside as the favoured tactic at many of the popular

Discovery Passage off Campbell River is a popular fishing area.

hotspots, increasing numbers of halibut have been appearing as incidental catches. Most come from around the Cape Mudge lighthouse and the deep water off Wilby Shoal. This leads us to believe that eventually dedicated halibut hunters will begin solving this area's mysteries, and anglers will actually start fishing for them intentionally. Time will tell.

Campbell River is dedicated to accommodating and servicing recreational anglers. The 45 km stretch from the Oyster River northwest to Brown Bay (including Quadra Island) offers over 30 resorts, hotels and motels, nine campgrounds and several bed and breakfast operations. There are 10 marinas, 11 boat rental operations, a dozen or so launch ramps, and a 600-foot-long fishing pier constructed specifically for that purpose.

Anglers lacking local information will usually do well to hire local guides or book stays at one of the area's fine resorts, all of which offer guided fishing packages.

For visitor information:

CAMPBELL RIVER VISITOR CENTRE
Box 400
1235 Shoppers Row
Campbell River, BC, V9W 5B6
(250) 286-4636
visitorinfo@campbellriverchamber.ca
www.visitorinfo.incampbellriver.com

Weather and Water Conditions

April and May in the Campbell River area are reasonably mild with occasional rain squalls, June is often unsettled and windy, and July through September is generally good. Nevertheless, always having rain gear available is a wise move.

Decent weather often continues until early October, then it's anyone's guess.

From the Oyster River mouth northwest to the top end of Duncan Bay, the shoreline is devoid of major tide rips and fast-flowing currents. This changes dramatically at Race Point, where the marine chart cautions that strong southerly winds and flood tides can form vicious tide rips. Believe it. It gets worse. Continuing northward through Seymour Narrows to Deepwater Bay should be attempted only by

The mouth of the Oyster River is the dividing line between Campbell River and the Comox Valley.

experienced boaters with seaworthy vessels. Considered one of the most treacherous stretches of navigable water on the West Coast, its tidal currents can exceed 25 kmh. At its worst there are long stretches of violent, white-capped rapids and standing waves, huge whirlpools, and cave-ins (sudden drops in water level) followed by surging upheavals.

If fishing along the western side of Quadra Island, use caution around the popular tide rips at Maud Island, Copper Cliffs, Whisky Point and Cape Mudge lighthouse for all can develop extremely rough

The Cape Mudge lighthouse on Quadra Island is a popular spot for chinooks but also yields occasional halibut.

water and occasional whirlpools. Discovery Passage is a major travel
route for large cruise ships, freighters, log carriers, tugboats and sein-
ers, and their passing often makes merely rough water downright
treacherous. Give these ships a wide berth and always watch for following waves.

Venturing offshore toward Sutil Point, Mitlenatch Island or
Montgomery Reef should be attempted only with reasonably fast, seaworthy boats equipped with a bare minimum of a working compass and
a VHF radio or cell phone. This vast, open area is subject to sudden
southeasters and northwesters, which can make things nasty. As the
weather cools, fog also becomes a considera-
tion, so having a GPS on board is recommended.

Guide's Tip:

Charter boats often attract other anglers
who figure that fishing close by will
improve their chances. It's a free country
and guides don't own the halibut, but
common sense dictates that setting up
too close to another boat can lead to
lines getting tangled if a fish is hooked.

Available Marine Charts:

3513 Strait of Georgia, Northern Portion
3538 Desolation Sound
3540 Approaches to Campbell River
3539 Discovery Passage and Seymour
Narrows

Marine Chart Coordinates:

Place Names:		Place Names:	
April Point	LAT 50°04′ LONG 125°14′	North Bluff	LAT 50°08′ LONG 125°21′
Big Rock	LAT 50°59¢ LONG 125°13′	Oyster River	LAT 49°52′ LONG 125°07′
Brown Bay	LAT 50°10′ LONG 125°22′	Plumper Point	LAT 50°10′ LONG 125°21′
Campbell River	LAT 50°02′ LONG 125°16′	Quadra Island	LAT 50°12′ LONG 125°15′
Campbell River C	LAT 50°01′ LONG 125°14′	Quathiaski Cove	LAT 50°03′ LONG 125°13′
Cape Mudge	LAT 50°00′ LONG 125°11′	Race Point	LAT 50°07′ LONG 125°20′
Copper Cliffs	LAT 50°06′ LONG 125°16′	Salmon Point	LAT 49°53′ LONG 125°07′
Deepwater Bay	LAT 50°11′ LONG 125°20′	Sentry Shoal	LAT 49°54′ LONG 124°59′
Discovery Passage	LAT 50°08′ LONG 125°21′	Seymour Narrows	LAT 50°09′ LONG 125°21′
Discovery Pier	LAT 50°02′ LONG 125°14′	Shelter Point	LAT 49°56′ LONG 125°11′
Duncan Bay	LAT 50°05′ LONG 125°18′	Steep Island	LAT 50°05′ LONG 125°15′
Francisco Point	LAT 50°01′ LONG 125°09′	Sutil Channel	LAT 50°08′ LONG 125°04′
Frenchman's Pool	LAT 50°03′ LONG 125°15′	Sutil Point	LAT 50°01′ LONG 124°59′
Gowlland Harbour	LAT 50°04′ LONG 125°13′	Tyee Pool	LAT 50°03′ LONG 125°15′
Gowlland Island	LAT 50°04′ LONG 125°14′	Tyee Spit	LAT 50°03′ LONG 125°15′
Kuhushan Point (Salmon Point)	LAT 49°53′ LONG 125°07′	Whisky Point	LAT 50°03′ LONG 125°13′
Marina Island	LAT 50°04′ LONG 125°03′	Wilby Shoals	LAT 50°59′ LONG 125°08′
Marina Reef	LAT 50°02′ LONG 125°03′	Wilfred Point (Green Light)	LAT 50°08′ LONG 125°21′
Maud Island	LAT 50°37′ LONG 125°36′	Willow Point	LAT 49°58′ LONG 125°12
Menzies Bay	LAT 50°07′ LONG 125°23′	Yaculta	LAT 50°01′ LONG 125°12′
Mitlenatch Island	LAT 49°57′ LONG 125°00′	Yellow Island	LAT 50°08′ LONG 125°19′
Montgomery Bank	LAT 49°54′ LONG 124°55′		

Many of the Comox Valley waters are suitable for small boats like this one used by Bill Rapanos to take his children, Stefan and Marika, out fishing.

COMOX VALLEY

The Comox Valley promotes itself as "The Outdoor Recreation Capital of Canada" because it offers one of the finest downhill and cross-country skiing areas in North America, 7 golf courses and 13 public tennis courts. Wind surfing, sailing and ocean kayaking are popular activities, and scuba divers claim that the waters off Denman and Hornby islands provide some of the most spectacular underwater scenery found anywhere in North America.

There are horse rentals for guided trail rides, and nearby Strathcona Park is crisscrossed with hiking trails, many leading to excellent rainbow trout fishing in the alpine lakes. Lower elevation lakes yield good catches of cutthroat and rainbow trout, and most rivers have seasonal runs of steelhead, sea-run cutthroat, plus chinook, coho, pink and chum salmon. The Puntledge River is also popular with rockhounds, fossil hunters, canoeists, and kayakers. Hunters have a good variety of big game at hand, plus upland game birds and several species of waterfowl.

Nevertheless, if the number of small boats observed at popular salmon haunts off the Comox Valley are any indication, saltwater fishing probably attracts more interest than all of the other outdoor activities combined. Angler success is no accident, for the area is centred between Campbell River and Qualicum Beach, both of which have efficient salmon hatcheries producing chinook and coho salmon. In addition, two hatcheries on the Puntledge River add several million juvenile salmon to the system annually. With so many anglers on the water, many of them downrigging deep and close to bottom, incidental catches of halibut have become fairly common.

There are several commercial and public launch ramps located throughout the area; these include Miracle Beach, Kitty Coleman Beach, Jasper's Resort, Bates Beach Resort, Point Holmes, Comox Marina, Royston, Union Bay, Fanny Bay and Hornby Island. Some resorts have boat rentals, and there are several experienced fishing guides available.

Weather and Water Conditions

The Comox Valley enjoys a moderate climate. April and May are fairly summer-like, but June often produces unsettled weather and windy conditions. July through September is usually decent, and even early October can be surprisingly summer-like. After that expect unsettled, typical West Coast weather until spring.

This is ideal water for small boats as there are no major tide rips or fast-flowing currents. You must always monitor wind conditions, however, for southeasters and northwesters can form quickly, creating problems for boaters trying to haul out at ramps located along an exposed shoreline. The Comox-Powell River ferry slip provides a good haven for waiting out a storm, and small boats can be beached there on the sloping, sandy shoreline. Another option is to head for Comox Harbour, which is protected by Goose Spit.

Venturing to offshore reefs, shoals and banks should be attempted only with reasonably fast, seaworthy boats, preferably with a GPS for operating in the fog conditions that usually start in early to mid-September.

Although there is no concentrated effort directed at halibut, as more anglers have switched to downrigging deeply for chinooks, incidental halibut catches have increased accordingly. Most are in the 20- to 40-pound range, but a few of 100-plus pounds have been reported. Halibut have been encountered virtually everywhere anglers fish for chinooks, most often in about 200 feet of water, and about 5-10 feet up from the bottom.

For visitor information:

227 COMOX VALLEY VISITOR CENTRE
2040 Cliffe Avenue
Courtenay, BC, V9N 2L3
(250) 334-3234
visitorinfo@comoxvalleychamber.com
www.comoxvalleychamber.com

Productive areas are along the drop-offs around Denman and Hornby islands, Ajax Bank, Exeter Shoal, Montgomery Bank and Grant Reefs. But before heading to any of these areas it is imperative that you check a current issue of the *BC Tidal Waters Sport Fishing Guide* for Rockfish Conservation Areas.

> **Guide's Tip:**
>
> When reeling up from the bottom, always stop at about the halfway point, let out 10 or 15 feet of line and start jigging. You won't hit a lot of fish this way, but it does happen on occasion.

Available Marine Charts:

3513 Strait of Georgia, Northern Portion
3527 Baynes Sound (Comox Harbour)

Marine Chart Coordinates:

Place Names:		Place Names:	
Ajax Bank	LAT 49°39′ LONG 124°43′	King Coho Resort	LAT 49°44′ LONG 124°54′
Bates Beach	LAT 49°46′ LONG 124°58′	Kitty Coleman Beach	LAT 49°47′ LONG 124°59′
Baynes Sound	LAT 49°29′ LONG 124°45′	Komass Bluff	LAT 49°35′ LONG 124°47′
Cape Gurney	LAT 49°31′ LONG 124°36′	Lambert Channel	LAT 49°30′ LONG 124°42′
Cape Lazo	LAT 49°42′ LONG 124°52′	Miracle Beach Prov. Park	LAT 49°51′ LONG 125°06′
Comox Harbour	LAT 49°40′ LONG 124°57′	Montgomery Bank	LAT 49°54′ LONG 124°55′
Denman Island	LAT 49°33′ LONG 124°48′	Palliser Rock	LAT 49°37′ LONG 124°50′
Exeter Shoal	LAT 49°39′ LONG 124°39′	Phipps Point	LAT 49°42′ LONG 124°43′
Favada Point	LAT 49°44′ LONG 124°38′	Seal Bay	LAT 49°46′ LONG 123°58′
Grant Reefs	LAT 49°53′ LONG 124°48′	Ship Point	LAT 49°30′ LONG 124°48′
Harwood Island	LAT 49°52′ LONG 124°39′	Vivian Island	LAT 49°50′ LONG 124°42′
Hornby Island	LAT 49°32′ LONG 124°40′	LAT 50°08′ LONG 125°19′	
Jasper's Resort	LAT 49°46′ LONG 124°58′		

NANAIMO AND THE GULF ISLANDS

Nanaimo—the Hub City—has a wide range of accommodations from which to choose, including hotels, motels, boatels, resorts and campgrounds. In addition, 11 marinas handle local boats as well as some extremely heavy transient marine traffic during the warm weather months. Most marinas operate on a first-come, first-served basis, but four are full all year.

The maze of over 200 islands, islets and channels located between Nanaimo and Sidney and known as the Gulf Islands is the most beautiful and interesting area in which to fish or cruise that can be found in the entire Strait of Georgia. While most destinations covered in this book have one major point of entry, the Gulf Islands can be accessed from Nanaimo, Ladysmith, Chemainus, Crofton, Maple Bay, Duncan (Cowichan Bay), Mill Bay and Sidney as well as Ganges and Fulford Harbour on Saltspring Island. All locations offer a range of accommodations and amenities so anglers may select whichever destination is closest to where they plan to fish. Those trailering boats can launch them at French Creek, Schooner Cove, Nanoose Bay, Lantzville or Nanaimo. Lower Mainland anglers with fast, seaworthy boats can reach the outer Gulf Islands by open water crossings of about 35 km from Vancouver or 20 km from Tsawwassen.

Weather and Water Conditions

Nanaimo and the Gulf Islands enjoy mild winters with slightly less precipitation than Vancouver. Spring, summer and fall are generally moderate, with July, August and September relatively free of rain.

For visitor information:

CHEMAINUS VISITOR CENTRE
9796 Willow Street
Box 575
Chemainus, BC, V0R 1K0
(250) 246-3944
www.chemainus.bc.ca

DUNCAN VISITOR CENTRE
381A Trans Canada Highway
Duncan, BC, V9L 3R5
(250) 748-1111
(888) 303-3337
www.duncan.bc.ca

GALIANO ISLAND TOURIST/VISITOR INFO
2590 Sturdies Bay Road (1 July-31 August)
Box 73
Galiano Island, BC, V0N 1P0
(250) 539-2233
(866) 539-2233
(250) 539-2507 (Off season)
www.galianoisland.com

LADYSMITH TOURIST/VISITOR INFO
132C Roberts Street
Box 98
Ladysmith, BC, V9G 1A4
(250) 245-2112
www.ladysmithcofc.com

NANAIMO VISITOR CENTRE
Beban House
2290 Bowen Road
Nanaimo, BC, V9T 3K7
(250) 756-0106
(800) 663-7337
www.tourismnanaimo.com

SALTSPRING ISLAND VISITOR CENTRE
121 Lower Ganges Road
Ganges, BC, V8K 2T1
(250) 537-5252
(866) 216-2936
www.saltspringtoday.com

SOUTH COWICHAN TOURIST/VISITOR INFO
Mill Bay Centre (18 May-4 September)
2720 Mill Bay Road
Mill Bay, BC, V0R 2P1
(250) 743-3566
info@southcowichanchamber.org

Five Finger Island off Nanaimo.

Like all open-water locations, the stretch from Nanaimo to Ballenas Channel, about 25 km northwest, is subject to variable weather conditions. From November to January strong southeasters are common, but those with seaworthy boats often find fishable water behind the islands clustered in Ballenas Channel. The use of caution and common sense is strongly recommended as is close monitoring of your VHF radio for warnings of worsening weather. The fairly predictable winter winds usually pose less danger than summer northwesters, which suddenly develop rough water conditions despite sunny, clear blue skies.

Anglers are catching halibut with increasing frequency in this area as they put in the time to discover their favoured habitats. Note that all the islands in the Ballenas Channel area are surrounded by rocks and reefs so you must carry a marine chart on board and monitor your depth sounder closely. However, the marine chart reveals many potential halibut spots in the Ballenas Channel to Nanoose Bay area, including the reef running from Pilot Bay to Entrance Island on the western end of Gabriola Island, and the sandy bottoms off the cliffs along the Gabriola side, which produce yelloweye rockfish and lingcod. Also check out the deeper areas off Entrance Island and Snake Island.

Winds seldom create problems inside the Gulf Islands cluster, but

Guide's Tip:

Whenever dogfish are present, switch to squid or octopus for bait. Those pesky little sharks won't eat these baits as quickly as they will salmon or herring.

outside waters are subject to prevailing Strait of Georgia winds and storms. From November to January strong southeasters are common, but fishable water can often be found in the lee of islands. Boaters crossing the Strait of Georgia between the Lower Mainland and Gulf Islands should maintain a sharp watch for summer northwesters. Late summer fog is also a fact of life, and combined with the profusion of islands can cause major confusion for boaters not prepared with a reliable compass and marine chart, and better yet, a GPS.

Most waters are safe for small boats, with notable exceptions being Active Pass, Nose Point in Captain Passage, Gabriola Passage, Race Point in Porlier Pass, and Dodd Narrows in Northumberland Channel. All develop swift currents and rough water conditions during peak tidal flows. Active Pass is also subject to heavy ferry traffic, and the Strait of Georgia side receives prevailing offshore winds, plus some rough tide rips during tide changes. While the inside waters of the Pass are relatively protected from offshore winds, you should give the ferry lanes a wide berth.

Because the Gulf Islands are so accessible from the Lower Mainland and southern Vancouver Island, they attract large numbers of salmon anglers. As a result, there is currently a permanent closure on Cowichan Bay, and seasonal spot closures in Active Pass, Porlier Pass, Yellow Point, Northumberland Channel, Chemainus River mouth, and Satellite Channel. Read the fishing regulations carefully before making plans.

When using a whole herring off a spreader bar or fish finder setup, rig it tail first on the tandem hooks. Fish always swallow bait headfirst.

Wherever you choose to fish, a typical bait rig to try over sandy, fairly smooth bottoms consists of a banana-shaped sinker heavy enough to get down and stay there, about three feet of leader, and a whole herring on a tandem hook setup. Drift jigs also work well, as do leadhead jigs with soft plastic bodies.

Available Marine Charts:

3310 Gulf Islands - Victoria Harbour to Nanaimo Harbour

3441 Haro Strait, Boundary Pass and Satellite Channel

3442 North Pender Island to Thetis Island

3443 Thetis Island to Nanaimo

3457 Nanaimo Harbour and Departure Bay.

3459 Approaches to Nanoose Harbour.

3458 Approaches to Nanaimo Harbour

3462 Juan de Fuca Strait to Strait of Georgia

3463 Strait of Georgia, Southern Portion

3475 Plans: Stuart Channel, Chemainus Bay, Ladysmith Harbour, Dodd Narrows to Flat Top Islands, Dodd Narrows,Osborn Bay

3476 Approaches to Tsehum Harbour

3477 Plans - Gulf Islands: Bedwell Harbour to Georgeson Passage, Telegraph Harbour and Preedy Harbour, Pender Canal

3478 Plans - Saltspring Island: Cowichan Bay to Maple Bay, Birds Eye Cove, Genoa Bay, Ganges Harbour and Long Harbour, Fulford Harbour

3512 Strait of Georgia, Central Portion

3463 Strait of Georgia, Southern Portion

Marine Chart Coordinates:

Place Names:		Place Names:	
Active Pass	LAT 48°53′ LONG 123°18′	Captain Passage	LAT 48°49′ LONG 123°24′
Active Point	LAT 48°57′ LONG 123°40′	Chemainus	LAT 48°55′ LONG 123°43′
Ada Islands	LAT 49°17′ LONG 124°05′	Cherry Point	LAT 48°43′ LONG 123°33′
Alarm Rock	LAT 48°57′ LONG 123°41′	Clarke Rock	LAT 49°13′ LONG 123°56′
Amelia Island	LAT 49°18′ LONG 124°09′	Coffin Point	LAT 48°59′ LONG 123°45′
Arbutus Point	LAT 48°49′ LONG 123°35′	Collinson Point	LAT 48°52′ LONG 123°21′
Augustus Point	LAT 48°57′ LONG 123°39′	Cottam Reef	LAT 49°19′ LONG 124°11′
Ballenas Channel	LAT 49°20′ LONG 124°10′	Crofton	LAT 48°52′ LONG 123°39′
Ballenas Islands	LAT 49°21′ LONG 124°09′	Danger Reefs	LAT 49°03′ LONG 123°43′
Bare Point	LAT 48°56′ LONG 123°42′	David Cove	LAT 48°51′ LONG 123°16′
Ben Mohr Rock	LAT 48°51′ LONG 123°23′	Davis Lagoon	LAT 48°57′ LONG 123°46′
Bird Rock	LAT 48°56′ LONG 123°43′	Dayman Island	LAT 48°58′ LONG 123°41′
Blunden Point	LAT 49°15′ LONG 124°05′	Deer Point	LAT 49°02′ LONG 123°46′
Boatswain Bank	LAT 48°42′ LONG 123°33′	Departure Bay	LAT 49°12′ LONG 123°57′
Bold Bluff Point	LAT 48°47′ LONG 123°33′	Dodd Narrows	LAT 49°08′ LONG 123°49′
Boulder Point	LAT 50°08′ LONG 124°54′	Donckele Point	LAT 48°58′ LONG 123°40′
Brant Reef	LAT 49°10′ LONG 124°40′	Dorcas Point	LAT 49°19′ LONG 124°11′
Burgoyne Bay	LAT 48°48′ LONG 123°32′	Dorcas Rock	LAT 49°19′ LONG 124°11′
Burial Islet	LAT 48°48′ LONG 123°32′	Douglas Island	LAT 49°19′ LONG 124°09′

Marine Chart Coordinates:

Place Names:		Place Names:	
Duncan	LAT 48°47' LONG 123°42'	Nanoose Bay	LAT 49°16' LONG 124°12'
Dunsmuir Islands	LAT 48°59' LONG 123°47'	Nanoose Harbour	LAT 49°16' LONG 124°10'
East Point	LAT 48°47' LONG 123°03'	Nares Rock	LAT 49°59' LONG 123°45'
Edgell Banks	LAT 49°16' LONG 124°03'	Narvaez Bay	LAT 48°46' LONG 123°06'
Enterprise Reef	LAT 48°51' LONG 123°21'	Neck Point	LAT 49°14' LONG 123°58'
Entrance Island	LAT 49°13' LONG 123°48'	North Reef	LAT 48°55' LONG 123°38'
Five Finger Island	LAT 49°14' LONG 123°55'	Northumberland Channel	LAT 49°09' LONG 123°51'
Flat Top Islands	LAT 49°09' LONG 123°41'	Nose Point	LAT 48°51' LONG 123°25'
Fleet Point	LAT 49°15' LONG 124°08'	Octopus Point	LAT 48048' LONG 123034'
Fraser Point	LAT 49°01' LONG 123°42'	Osborn Bay	LAT 48°52' LONG 123°38'
Fulford Harbour	LAT 48°46' LONG 123°26'	Paddy Mile Stone	LAT 48°49' LONG 123°25'
Gabriola Island	LAT 49°10' LONG 123°48'	Pilkey Point	LAT 49°01' LONG 123°41'
Gabriola Passage	LAT 49°08' LONG 123°43'	Pilot Bay	LAT 49°12' LONG 123°51'
Ganges	LAT 48°51' LONG 123°30'	Porlier Pass	LAT 49°01' LONG 123°35'
Genoa Bay	LAT 48°46' LONG 123°36'	Race Point	LAT 49°01' LONG 123°35'
Georgina Point	LAT 48°52' LONG 123°17'	Ragged Islets	LAT 49°02' LONG 123°41'
Georgina Shoals	LAT 48°52' LONG 123°17'	Rainbow Channel	LAT 49°14' LONG 123°53'
Gerald Island	LAT 49°19' LONG 124°10'	Rosenfeld Rock	LAT 48°48' LONG 123°02'
Gossip Island	LAT 48°53' LONG 123°19'	Round Island	LAT 49°07' LONG 123°48'
Gossip Shoals	LAT 48°53' LONG 123°18'	Rudder Rock	LAT 49°17' LONG 124°04'
Grave Point	LAT 48°51' LONG 123°35'	Ruth Island	LAT 49°18' LONG 124°08'
Grey Rock	LAT 49°17' LONG 124°04'	Saltspring Island	LAT 48°45' LONG 123°29'
Helen Point	LAT 48°51' LONG 123°21'	Sandstone Rocks	LAT 48°55' LONG 123°37'
Holland Bank	LAT 48°59' LONG 123°48'	Sansum Narrows	LAT 48°48' LONG 123°34'
Horswell Channel	LAT 49°13' LONG 123°56'	Satellite Channel	LAT 48°43' LONG 123°26'
Hospital Point	LAT 48°56' LONG 123°43'	Saturna Island	LAT 48°47' LONG 123°09'
Hospital Rock	LAT 48°56' LONG 123°43'	Schooner Cove	LAT 49°04' LONG 124°48'
Houstoun Passage	LAT 48°56' LONG 123°36'	Scott Island	LAT 48°58' LONG 123°42'
Hudson Rocks	LAT 49°13' LONG 123°55'	Separation Point	LAT 48°44' LONG 123°34'
Hudson Island	LAT 48°58' LONG 123°41'	Sharpe Point	LAT 49°21' LONG 126°16'
Icarus Point	LAT 49°15' LONG 124°02'	Sherard Point	LAT 48°52' LONG 123°37'
Josling Point	LAT 48°56' LONG 123°38'	Sidney	LAT 48°39' LONG 123°24'
Kulleet Bay	LAT 49°01' LONG 123°46'	Snake Island	LAT 49°13' LONG 123°53'
Kuper Island	LAT 48°58' LONG 123°39'	Southey Island	LAT 49°17' LONG 124°06'
Ladysmith	LAT 48°59' LONG 123°49'	Stuart Channel	LAT 49°00' LONG 123°42'
Ladysmith Harbour	LAT 49°00' LONG 123°48'	Telegraph Cove	LAT 48°28' LONG 123°17'
Lantzville	LAT 49°15' LONG 124°04'	Tent Island	LAT 48°56' LONG 123°38'
Lion Islets	LAT 48°54' LONG 123°20'	Thetis Island	LAT 49°00' LONG 123°41'
Maple Bay	LAT 48°49' LONG 123°36'	Thrasher Rock	LAT 49°09' LONG 123°39'
Mary Anne Point	LAT 48°52' LONG 123°19'	Trincomali Channel	LAT 48°58' LONG 123°35'
Maude Island	LAT 49°16' LONG 124°05'	Tumbo Reef	LAT 48°48' LONG 123°03'
Maxwell Point	LAT 48°49' LONG 123°34'	Valdes Island	LAT 49°05' LONG 123°40'
Miami Islet	LAT 49°02' LONG 123°42'	Vesuvius Bay	LAT 48°53' LONG 123°34'
Mill Bay	LAT 48°39' LONG 123°33'	Village Bay	LAT 48°51' LONG 123°19'
Miners Bay	LAT 48°51' LONG 123°18'	Whaler Bay	LAT 48°53' LONG 123°20'
Mistaken Island	LAT 49°20' LONG 124°13'	Winchelsea Islands	LAT 49°18' LONG 124°05'
Monarch Head	LAT 48°46' LONG 123°06'	Yellow Point	LAT 49°02' LONG 123°45'
Montague Harbour	LAT 48°53' LONG 123°24'	Yeo Islands	LAT 49°18' LONG 124°08'
Nanaimo	LAT 49°10' LONG 123°56'		

West Coast Destinations
QUATSINO SOUND

When weather conditions get nasty on Queen Charlotte Strait, many Port Hardy anglers simply haul out and trailer their boats about 16 km west to Coal Harbour in order to go fishing in Quatsino Sound. The most northerly of five major sounds on the west coast of Vancouver Island, Quatsino cleaves northeast from Cliffe Point on the west coast for 30 km to Quatsino Narrows where it branches out in three directions. Just before the Narrows entrance Neroutsos Inlet swings southeast for 20 km past Jeune Landing, Port Alice, and the huge Neucel Specialty Cellulose pulp mill. Just beyond the Narrows, Rupert Inlet continues northeast for 10 km, past what was once the third largest copper mine in Canada, the Island Copper Mine, a truly massive hole in the ground that is now flooded. Holberg Inlet also begins at Quatsino Narrows and cuts almost 35 km west to the community of Holberg, once the site of the world's largest floating logging camp. Later it became a Royal Canadian Air Force radar station, part of the North American Air Defence (NORAD) system. The combined length of this roughly X-shaped network of water totals about 100 km,

Quatsino Narrows is well protected from offshore winds and rough water.

and being surrounded by steep mountains means that it is fairly well protected from offshore winds.

Coal Harbour is a docking and fuelling area for commercial fishing vessels, logging company tugs and crew boats, and the boats that service the local aquaculture operations. There is a private launch ramp and parking lot located right beside an old seaplane hangar; you pay for your launch at the Air Cab office. The wide gravel ramp has a moderate pitch so launching large boats is best accomplished at the top half of high tide. Space is limited at the private wharf and the small government wharf is usually filled to capacity with commercial fishing vessels.

As well as the road from Port Hardy to Coal Harbour, Quatsino Sound is also accessible by a 42 km gravel road west from Port Hardy to Holberg then 25 km south to Winter Harbour. But be warned that these are active logging roads. Koprino Harbour, 33 km southeast of Holberg, is about midway between Quatsino Narrows and the mouth of Quatsino Sound. There you will find the Spencer Cove Recreation Site, which is co-managed by the BC Forest Service and Western Forest Products. It has a ramp suitable for small boats, a docking area, and 11 campsites.

Near the mouth of Quatsino Sound, Forward Inlet is tucked in behind Cape Parkins. It curves northward into the well-protected waters of Winter Harbour, where most of the residents are involved with commercial fishing, forestry, or the tourism industry. The most western community in North America, it has a unique network of wooden boardwalks connecting the houses and buildings that are located along its shoreline—a reminder of times prior to the 1970s when it was accessible only by boat or floatplane.

The 12-site Kwaksistah Campground, operated by the District of Mount Waddington, is located about 1 km north of the community. The nearby boat launch is best used at high tide. Among the accommodations available are Dick's Last Resort, which also has cabins; Frosty's Winter Harbour with two floating cabins; The Outpost at Winter Harbour with RV sites, waterfront suites, moorage, a full service marina and a well-stocked general store; and the recently built Qualicum Rivers Fishing Resort. The latter two offer fishing packages with experienced, fully equipped guides.

For visitor information:

PORT HARDY VISITOR INFO CENTRE
7250 Market Street
Box 249
Port Hardy, BC, V0N 2P0
(250) 949-7622
phcc@cablerocket.com
www.ph-chamber.bc.ca

For fair weather fishing within the confines of Quatsino Sound and the inlets, boats of 14 to 16 feet are suitable. The absolute minimum navigational requirements are a marine chart, compass and depth sounder. For offshore fishing, where high swells and choppy conditions are common, think in terms of at least 20 feet long, and to your navigational aids add a VHF radio, GPS, and radar to cope with the fog.

Weather and Water Conditions

Although the North Island's annual rainfall averages about 250-300 cm, Quatsino Sound is in a rain shadow so somewhat drier. Nevertheless, appropriate wet weather clothing is recommended. Most heavy rains occur from November through February, but even then there are occasional stretches of moderate, dry weather.

May or June can be unsettled with offshore westerlies blowing about 25 kmh, but during summer highs, occasional storm force winds are southeasters, which can be nasty.

Fog is relatively rare around Coal Harbour and Quatsino Narrows during the winter months. Out near the mouth of the Sound, however, where it faces the open Pacific, fog definitely becomes a fact of life during warm weather.

If conditions permit fishing in the exposed waters, the sand banks located 3 to 5 km off Kains Island lighthouse are considered the "chicken coop" but a few big halibut are also caught there. Bait is often concentrated around the rock piles in 100 to 150 feet of water where fast currents are found, and these are often the areas where larger-than-average halibut are hooked.

During the summer, halibut do migrate inland as far as Quatsino Narrows, where a good supply of food washes through in the strong current. Try for them off Koprino Harbour, around Monday Rocks, and across the inlet in Koskimo Bay, right off the Mahatta River mouth. Be aware that it is mostly a mud bottom there, which the halibut avoid, so look around until you locate the clean gravel bottom.

The rockfish assortment, which is far more varied than on the eastern coast of Vancouver Island, includes

Guide's Tip:

Always give the fish a choice of bait or lures. Whenever I'm fishing four rods there are always four different-coloured jigs down, and if I'm using bait there will be an assortment of herring, salmon, octopus or squid.

yelloweye, redstripe, canary, quillback, black, and possibly some of the largest vermilion rockfish found on the West Coast.

Available Marine Charts:

3617 Quatsino Sound
3681 Plans Quatsino Sound: Coal Harbour, Quatsino Narrows, Neroutsos Inlet, Port Alice

Marine Chart Coordinates:

Place Names:		Place Names:	
Brown Rock	LAT 50°27′ LONG 127°59′	Kultus Cove	LAT 50°29′ LONG 127°37′
Cape Parkins	LAT 50°27′ LONG 128°03′	Kwakiutl Point	LAT 50°21′ LONG 127°59′
Cliffe Point	LAT 50°28′ LONG 128°56′	Marble River	LAT 50°32′ LONG 127°31′
Coal Harbour	LAT 50°36′ LONG 127°35′	McAllister Islet	LAT 50°28′ LONG 127°59′
Drake Island	LAT 50°30′ LONG 127°40′	Monday Rocks	LAT 50°29′ LONG 127°53′
Forward Inlet	LAT 50°30′ LONG 128°02′	Neroutsos Inlet	LAT 50°24′ LONG 127°31′
Gillam Islands	LAT 50°27′ LONG 127°58′	Port Alice	LAT 50°23′ LONG 127°27′
Gooding Cove	LAT 50°24′ LONG 127°57′	Quatsino Narrows	LAT 50°33′ LONG 127°34′
Goodspeed River	LAT 50°39′ LONG 128°01′	Quatsino Sound	LAT 50°30′ LONG 127°35′
Grant Bay	LAT 50°28′ LONG 128°05′	Restless Bight	LAT 50°22′ LONG 127°58′
Harvey Cove	LAT 50°26′ LONG 127°55′	Robson Rock	LAT 50°26′ LONG 128°01′
Hathaway Creek	LAT 50°35′ LONG 127°46′	Rowley Reefs	LAT 50°24′ LONG 127°58′
Hecate Cove	LAT 50°33′ LONG 127°36′	Rupert Inlet	LAT 50°35′ LONG 127°30′
Holberg	LAT 50°39′ LONG 128°01′	South Danger Rock	LAT 50°26′ LONG 128°00′
Holberg Inlet	LAT 50°36′ LONG 127°44′	Spencer Cove Recreation Site	LAT 50°30′ LONG 127°52′
Jeune Landing	LAT 50°26′ LONG 127°29′	Stephens Creek	LAT 50°36′ LONG 127°34′
Kains Island	LAT 50°27′ LONG 128°02′	Winter Harbour	LAT 50°32′ LONG 128°00′
Koprino Harbour	LAT 50°30′ LONG 127°51′	Waukwaas Creek	LAT 50°35′ LONG 127°25′
Koskimo Bay	LAT 50°28′ LONG 127°53′		

ZEBALLOS AND KYUQUOT SOUND

The west coast of Vancouver Island attracts tens of thousands of salt-water anglers each year, often resulting in crowded fishing conditions at most of the more popular, road accessible locations. One, however, that has an excellent catch record yet remains relatively uncrowded is Zeballos, although this is changing as the area's excellent fishing prospects gain wider recognition. Another is Kyuquot Sound, which requires driving 34 km beyond Zeballos to Fair Harbour, and then making a boat trip of about 30 minutes.

Visitors driving to Zeballos and Fair Harbour must turn left off Highway 19 about 20 km northwest of Woss, then travel south for 42 km over a well-signed but winding and extremely dusty gravel road. This is an active logging road, so you must remain constantly alert to

The harbour at Zeballos has fuel, moorage and a launch ramp with limited parking.

oncoming traffic. Keep your speed down as there are plenty of hills and all of them have washboard surfaces. Your vehicle windows should be up and tightly sealed, and your air conditioner or heater fan on high. If towing a boat and motor, cover them tightly beforehand for dust protection and carry at least one spare tire for your boat trailer.

Although Zeballos receives thousands of visitors every summer, saltwater and freshwater anglers are actually a small percentage. Most are nature lovers, outdoor enthusiasts, ocean kayakers or people interested in the village's history. The name of both village and inlet honours Lieutenant Ciriaco Cevallos, a Spaniard who explored the inlet in 1791. The Spanish discovered gold there and successfully mined it, but when they ceded the region to England, the presence of gold remained their secret. After prospectors again discovered gold during the early 1900s, mining began in the 1920s, and the townsite emerged during the mid-1930s. Although inaccessible by road, it offered most of the amenities and services, including hotels, well-stocked stores, a bank, school and library, and by 1939 the population was over 1,500. The Second World War drained the mines of skilled labour and by 1943 they had all closed. They reopened in 1945, but with gold pegged at $35 an ounce, they were no longer viable so closed again in 1948.

An iron mine that opened in the early 1960s was short lived, and by 1970 the population had dropped to 35. Zeballos received a new lease on life when the Tahsis Logging Company established its headquarters there in 1969, and construction of a road finally made it accessible by means other than boat or floatplane. Although logging is still the area's major employer, aquaculture and tourism are now important contributors to the economy.

The population of Zeballos now hovers around 260. It has 5 motor lodges and a hotel, a general store with a liquor outlet and gas pumps, coin laundry, gift shops and a museum. There is an excellent all-tide boat ramp with adjacent parking, a government wharf, moorage and a fuel dock. There is a campsite located about 7 km north of Zeballos, the Cevallos campsite right in town, and the BCFS Rhodes Creek campsite about 7 km south of town on the road to Fair Harbour. This well-shaded site also has a launch ramp and a small dock. If you are camping, be aware that this area has a healthy population of black bears so take the necessary precautions to prevent encounters.

Weather and Water Conditions

Aside from occasional windy stretches, the weather is generally pleasant from May until October, when it turns wet and windy. This pretty well sums up the winter weather, and while there are occasional stretches of nice days, they can't be forecast. Although spring conditions start around early March, don't expect much good weather until mid-April.

While Zeballos Inlet is well protected, the mouth of Esperanza Inlet is exposed to the open Pacific, subjecting it to the whims of offshore wave action that can range from flat calm to downright dangerous. During summer months the prevailing winds are usually southerlies—southeast or southwest. The wind and water conditions may remain unsettled until early June when they usually level out until mid- to late September. Morning fog can be a problem during this warm-weather period, but it usually burns off before noon.

Halibut fishing can be quite good during the early spring when they come close inshore to spawn, in some cases almost right into the inlets.

Pin Rock is located on the southeast side of Gillam Channel, near the mouth of Esperanza Inlet

After this they move farther offshore for the summer, but if the weather cooperates you can run up to 10 km offshore to where the marine chart shows a flat, sandy area at 36 to 40 m. The usual array of spreader bars and top-rigged jigs produce, but many of the locals swear by large Buzz Bombs. Some of the halibut hit 100-plus pounds, so go prepared.

There are good populations of bottom fish here and locating them is usually just a matter of matching the bottom structure to the species sought. There are plenty of black and China rockfish around the kelp beds, greenling and lingcod near the pinnacles and rock piles, and yelloweye and vermilion rockfish in the deeper water. It's still possible to connect with lingcod of 40-plus pounds in some of these areas.

Guide's Tip:

When fishing braided GSP main line, use a 3- to 5-foot length of 100- to 150-pound test monofilament leader between the main line and lure or spreader bar. This helps alleviate the constant tangling of the softer braid lines, and is easier on your hand if it's necessary to grab the line while positioning a fish beside the boat.

Available Marine Charts:

L/C 3604 Nootka Sound to Quatsino Sound
3663 Esperanza Inlet

Marine Chart Coordinates:

Place Names:		Place Names:	
Black Rock	LAT 49°50' LONG 127°02'	Nuchatlitz Reef	LAT 49°46' LONG 126°59'
Blind Reef	LAT 49°47' LONG 127°01'	Obstruction Reef	LAT 49°50' LONG 127°05'
Brodick Creek	LAT 49°51' LONG 126°54'	Outer Black Rock	LAT 49°49' LONG 127°04'
Catala Island	LAT 49°50' LONG 127°03'	Peculiar Point	LAT 49°51' LONG 127°06'
Centre Island	LAT 49°51' LONG 126°56'	Pin Rock	LAT 49°47' LONG 127°00'
Danger Rock	LAT 49°49' LONG 126°59'	Port Eliza	LAT 49°53' LONG 127°01'
Esperanza	LAT 49°52' LONG 126°44'	Queen Cove	LAT 49°53' LONG 126°59'
Ferrer Point	LAT 49°45' LONG 126°59'	Rolling Roadstead	LAT 49°51' LONG 127°03'
Gillam Channel	LAT 49°48' LONG 127°01'	Rosa Island	LAT 49°50' LONG 126°58'
Halftide Reef	LAT 49°50' LONG 127°05'	Steamer Point	LAT 49°43' LONG 126°48'
Kaouk River	LAT 50°04' LONG 127°06'	Tahsis	LAT 49°55' LONG 126°40'
Kyuquot Sound	LAT 50°04' LONG 127°13'	Tahsish River	LAT 50°09' LONG 127°06'
Little Zeballos	LAT 49°57' LONG 126°49'	Tatchu Point	LAT 49°51' LONG 127°09'
Low Rock	LAT 49°48' LONG 127°04'	Yellow Bluff	LAT 49°51' LONG 127°07'
Middle Reef	LAT 49°48' LONG 127°02'	Zeballos	LAT 49°59' LONG 126°51
Nootka Island	LAT 49°45' LONG 127°45'	Zeballos Inlet	LAT 49°57' LONG 126°49'
Nuchatlitz Inlet	LAT 49°46' LONG 126°56'	Zeballos River	LAT 49°59' LONG 126°51'

KYUQUOT SOUND

Kyuquot Sound can be accessed only by air or water. Air Nootka offers regular scheduled flights from Gold River as well as charter flights all year, and Vancouver Island Air sends almost daily charter flights from Campbell River during the summer months. An option that some find adventuresome and interesting is to book passage out of Gold River on the MV *Uchuck III*, a passenger-carrying coastal freighter that makes scheduled two-day trips to Kyuquot, departing on Thursdays and returning on Fridays.

However, most visitors get to Kyuquot Sound by continuing beyond Zeballos for another 34 km of gravel road to Fair Harbour. The turnoff is at the bridge spanning the Zeballos River as you drive into Zeballos, but I recommend that, before you go on to Fair Harbour, you drive into Zeballos and gas up your vehicle, for while propane, marine gas and diesel are available at Fair Harbour, no vehicle gas is sold there. Although the road from Zeballos to Fair Harbour isn't any better than that from Highway 19 to Zeballos, it is an interesting and pleasant drive through some very scenic country, and you will probably encounter black bears and black-tailed deer and possibly some Roosevelt elk along the way.

At Fair Harbour you will find a Forest Service campsite, unpaved boat launch (free), government dock, fuel dock (diesel, marine gas and propane), public parking, and the Swan Song Marina, which offers some moorage and 6 private campsites with fresh water and outhouses. Two of these sites are large enough to handle groups. In addition, there is secure parking on the upper level but it is usually booked up early in the season as is the moorage.

Marina owners Gail and Richard Leo also operate a general store that offers basic groceries, camping supplies, souvenirs and, amazingly enough, fishing tackle that is often cheaper than you will find it priced elsewhere. They don't always have frozen bait on hand because they need the freezer space to keep campers supplied with ice. They are open year round and usually expect to see some of the more avid

You seldom need to fish far out of Kyuquot Sound to find halibut action.

For visitor information:

KYUQUOT CHECLESET BAND OFFICE
Kyuquot, BC, V0P 1J0
Bus: (250) 332-5259
Fax: (250) 332-5210

halibut anglers as early as April. This is a great place to drop in to find out which baits and lures are working best and to determine where the best fishing action has been occurring.

Most of those who tow their own boats to Fair Harbour usually camp there as Kyuquot Sound is only a half-hour run from the dock. Those without boats should have arranged beforehand to be picked up by one of the fishing resorts or water taxies located on the Sound. There are several fishing lodges and assorted bed-and-breakfast operations in the area and a few cabins are available for rent.

Those interested in camping must do some homework ahead of time. There are 5 marine provincial parks in the area: Big Bunsby (658 ha), Brooks Peninsula (51,631 ha), Dixie Cove (156 ha), Rugged Point (308 ha), and Tahsish-Kwois (10,972 ha). The Kyuquot and Checleset bands, northernmost of the 14 Nuu-chah-nulth First Nation bands, control access to many of their traditional territories, so visitors must register at the Kyuquot Checleset Band Office in Houpsitas before venturing onto any of them. In the village of Fair Harbour itself, Mike and Suzy Bostrom operate Kyuquot Market, a small, well-stocked general store that also supplies ice, bait and fishing gear. The only eatery is Miss Charlie's Restaurant, which is named after Kyuquot's famous pet seal.

Being located on the migration path of salmon runs heading south for Nootka Sound and as far south as the Columbia River, Kyuquot Sound attracts chinook anglers during June, July and August, after which the coho action heats up until well into September. This is obviously when halibut get the most attention, but those interested in specifically targeting them start showing up as early as April and some continue to visit until winter storms get too unruly.

Weather and Water Conditions

Although spring conditions might begin to develop in early March, most halibut anglers don't plan their early trips until mid- to late April. However, wind and water conditions may remain unsettled into early June, after which they are usually more co-operative until mid- to late September. Aside from occasional high winds, the weather is generally pleasant from May until October when it turns wet and windy. Heavy rains occur from November through February although they are interspaced with stretches of moderate, dry weather.

The open Pacific ranges anywhere from flat calm to thoroughly dangerous. During the summer months the prevailing winds are usually southerlies—southeast or southwest. Morning fog can be a problem during this warm-weather period, but it usually burns off before noon.

Guide's Tip:

When bottom-bouncing with multiple lines, rig at least one with a large bait such as a whole salmon head or whole mackerel. The old equation "big bait equals big fish" often proves true.

Kyuquot could well be the most rock-filled sound on the Island's west coast, and running into one of these rocks can quickly ruin a fishing trip. It is strongly advised that you either hire a guide or travel with someone who has fished there before and knows the area well.

While much of the fishing is fairly close to shore and around the kelp beds, whenever the open Pacific is co-operative, those with fast, seaworthy boats can run out to a reef about 15 km from the Mission Group of islands. Located in about 200 feet of water, this reef rises up fairly sharply to within 100 feet of the surface. Depending on your location while out on the water, in addition to the usual assortment of sea birds and ducks, you might see puffins, pigeon guillemots, rhinoceros auklets and an occasional albatross gliding in from beyond the continental shelf. Sea otters are now fairly common throughout the area as are sea lions and grey whales.

If the islands off Rugged Point don't produce, try the Thornton Islands, where the presence of herring attracts salmon and bottom fish. Another spot is "The Wall" near Racoon Point, located out from Union Island, where the shallow bottom drops sharply to 120 feet. In addition to halibut there are good populations of rockfish, including yelloweye, redstripe, canary, quillback, black, China and vermilion. Lingcod are also common, with some in the 30- to 40-pound range although, as these are spawning-age females, anglers usually release them.

Available Marine Charts:

3604 Nootka Sound to Quatsino Sound
3623 Kyuquot Sound to Cape Cook
3682 Kyuquot Sound

Marine Chart Coordinates:

Place Names:		Place Names:	
Big Bunsby MPP	LAT 50°06' LONG 127°30'	Mission Group	LAT 50°00' LONG 127°24'
Brooks Peninsula MPP	LAT 50°10' LONG 127°45'	Racoon Point	LAT 49°59' LONG 127°18'
Checleset Bay	LAT 50°06' LONG 127°40'	Rugged Point MPP	LAT 49°58' LONG 127°15'
Clanninick Creek	LAT 50°03' LONG 127°24'	Solander Island	LAT 50°07' LONG 127°56'
Copp Island	LAT 50°03' LONG 127°11'	Spring Island	LAT 50°00' LONG 127°25'
Dixie Cove MPP	LAT 50°03' LONG 127°12'	Tahsish River	LAT 50°09' LONG 127°06'
Fair Harbour	LAT 50°04' LONG 127°07'	Tahsish-Kwois MPP	LAT 50°06' LONG 127°07'
Hohoae Island	LAT 50°03' LONG 127°13'	Thornton Islands	LAT 49°58' LONG 127°20'
Houpsitas	LAT 50°02' LONG 127°22'	Thornton Reef	LAT 50°56' LONG 127°46'
Kyuquot Channel	LAT 49°59' LONG 127°15'	Union Island	LAT 50°01' LONG 127°16'
Kyuquot Sound	LAT 50°04' LONG 127°13'		

*Note: MPP is Marine Provincial Park.

NOOTKA SOUND

Long before the "instant town" of Gold River was established in 1965, saltwater anglers used a network of gravel logging roads from Campbell River to make their way to Muchalat Inlet in search of big chinook salmon. Today access is by Highway 28, a scenic route that borders Upper Campbell Lake before it swings westward at Buttle Narrows. The village offers a full range of accommodations and services as well as several fishing charter companies.

About 13 km past the village at the mouth of Gold River is a well-maintained concrete launch ramp. It gets extremely crowded here from

The lighthouse on Nootka Island at the mouth of Nootka Sound.

mid-July through August, and break-ins and vandalism to vehicles and trailers have been reported at this site. The run westward from here down Muchalat Inlet to Friendly Cove is about 39 km. Favour the north side, passing Gore Island through Williamson Passage, then bear left through Zuciarte Channel to reach Nootka Sound.

Increasing numbers of anglers now continue driving past Gold River toward Tahsis, which is slightly over 60 km away on an often dusty but fairly well-maintained gravel road. Note that this is an active logging road and drive accordingly. Some head for the BC Forest Service campsite at Cougar Creek on Tlupana Inlet, others for Moutcha Bay Resort, which also has an RV park, cabins, a chalet and marina.

Tahsis has a full range of services and accommodations, including a motel, RV park and a few bed and breakfasts. Westview Marina has a fairly large dock. A bit farther down the main street is a concrete launch ramp but parking is quite limited. The run southward down Tahsis Inlet to Friendly Cove is 38 km. Tahsis is also the departure point for several remote lodges located throughout the Nootka Sound region, some land-based, others on floats, and one on Nootka Island. All can also be reached by water from Gold River or by floatplane.

The BC Forest Service campsite at Cougar Creek has 18 sites and a rough launch ramp suitable for small boats. To get there, take the Nesook Bay turnoff and follow it about 6 km to the log dump, then follow the Tlupana road another 8 km to the campsite. There are reports that during late July and August upward of 200 vehicles, most with boat trailers, have been jammed into the area and strung out along the road.

About 15 km past the Tlupana Bay turnoff you will find the well-marked short access road to Moutcha Bay Marina and RV Park located near the mouth of the Conuma River. This marina has a wide gravel launch ramp capable of handling large boats although anything over 20 feet might have to wait for an incoming tide.

Yet another option for travelling to Nootka Sound is booking

A bird's-eye view of Tlupana Inlet. (Charlie Cornfield photo)

passage out of Gold River on the MV *Uchuck III*, a passenger-carrying coastal freighter that makes scheduled day trips to Tahsis on Mondays, Friendly Cove on Wednesdays, two-day trips to Kyuquot on Thursdays and Fridays, and unscheduled chartered sailings on Mondays and Saturdays. Campers with small boats can arrange to have their equipment loaded aboard, be dropped off at a predetermined destination and picked up on a return trip.

Several islands and small coves throughout Nootka Sound are suitable for camping. The main considerations are a gently sloping beach where boats can be beached or securely anchored and a level place to pitch a tent. As fresh water might not be available, take containers. Remember, too, that this is black bear country and take precautions to prevent encounters.

In addition to the area's salmon and bottom fishing, there is excellent crabbing and prawning, plus clams and oysters galore. Including a trap or two, a small rake and a shucking knife in your equipment will help provide some outstanding seafood meals.

Weather and Water Conditions

Winter weather on Nootka Sound is generally wet, windy and unpredictable, and water conditions range from uncomfortably lumpy to "don't even consider it." There are often a few respites between January and April but you cannot count on them. Although the weather starts to improve in April, wind and water conditions can continue swinging from bad to good right on through June. While July, August and early

September are usually quite reasonable, fog can be a problem, especially during the morning hours. During clear, sunny weather, thermal winds make things rough, so plan on early morning starts and get off the water for midday. Things usually calm down by late afternoon, so there is good evening fishing.

A line from Yuquot Point to Burdwood Point marks the difference between Nootka Sound's "outside" and "inside" fishing areas. Outside, summer westerlies are seldom a problem for seaworthy boats but southerlies can be dangerous. Fortunately, the inside has plenty of protected areas that provide comfortable fishing conditions during heavy blows outside.

As elsewhere along Vancouver Island's west coast, high swells from the open Pacific are fairly consistent and if a cross-chop develops there are more pleasant places to be than in a boat. Anyone venturing outside or offshore should be experienced and should do so only in seaworthy boats with suitable navigation and communication equipment.

Halibut are caught here all year but the prime time is April and May, which also happens to be a good time to see grey whales on their northward migration. It is not necessary to take long runs offshore to find halibut for they are often in close all the way from Bajo Reef to Maquinna Point and on past Wash Rock to Yuquot. Discovery Point, Burdwood Point and Escalante Rocks can also be good. Virtually any location with a deep, flat, sandy bottom encircling islands, rocks or reefs should be considered potential halibut water. On the inside try Zuciarte Channel, around the Spanish Pilot Group and along the west side of Bligh Island.

To locate halibut here, try downrigging with large white or green/white hoochies or with light-coloured Tomic Plugs. Once halibut

Deep trolling a Tomic Plug allows the angler to cover much more water than jigging or bottom bouncing.

Green/white is the favourite hoochie colour combination for all species of fish.

Guide's Tip:

When fishing spreader bars with bait, use sliding tandem hooks. Unlike standard tandem hook setups, the sliding top hook allows you to properly rig baits of different sizes, creating a better presentation.

are found, they can be taken with herring, squid, octopus or strips of salmon belly fished on the bottom or with heavy top-rigged jigs or drift jigs.

There is a good selection of rockfish, including some of the largest vermilions on the coast (12-plus pounds), yelloweyes, browns, blacks, Chinas, and red stripes. It is still possible to catch big lingcod of 40-plus pounds here, but most anglers release them in favour of smaller, tastier fish. Drift-jigging along Wash Rock works well for lingcod as does trolling a green hoochie or mooching a 10-inch long green plastic worm (honest!).

Available Marine Charts:

3603 Ucluelet Inlet to Nootka Sound
3604 Nootka Sound to Quatsino Sound
3662 Nootka Sound to Esperanza Inlet
3664 Nootka Sound

Marine Chart Coordinates:

Place Names:		Place Names:	
Anderson Point	LAT 49°39' LONG 126°28'	Hanna Channel	LAT 49°40' LONG 126°29'
Bajo Reef	LAT 49°34' LONG 126°49'	Head Bay	LAT 49°48' LONG 126°29'
Bligh Island	LAT 49°39' LONG 126°32'	Hesquiat Peninsula	LAT 49°24' LONG 126°30'
Burdwood Point	LAT 49°35' LONG 126°34'	King Passage	LAT 49°38' LONG 126°23'
Burman River	LAT 49°37' LONG 126°03'	Maquinna Point	LAT 49°35' LONG 126°40'
Camel Rock	LAT 49°41' LONG 126°30'	Moutcha Bay	LAT 49°47' LONG 126°27'
Canton Creek	LAT 49°48' LONG 126°28'	Muchalat Inlet	LAT 49°39' LONG 126°14'
Clerke Peninsula	LAT 49°37' LONG 126°31'	Nesook Bay	LAT 49°46' LONG 126°25'
Concepcion Point	LAT 49°40' LONG 126°29'	Nootka Sound	LAT 49°36' LONG 126°34'
Conuma River	LAT 49°48' LONG 126°26'	Princess Royal Point	LAT 49°45' LONG 126°27'
Cook Channel	LAT 49°38' LONG 126°36'	Saavedra Islands	LAT 49°37' LONG 126°37'
Descubierta Point	LAT 49°41' LONG 126°30'	San Carlos Point	LAT 49°41' LONG 126°31'
Discovery Point	LAT 49°35' LONG 126°33'	Spanish Pilot Group	LAT 49°38' LONG 126°35'
Escalante Point	LAT 49°32' LONG 126°34'	Tahsis	LAT 49°55' LONG 126°40'
Escalante Rocks	LAT 49°32' LONG 126°35'	Tlupana Inlet	LAT 49°43' LONG 126°28'
Ewin Inlet	LAT 49°38' LONG 126°32'	Verdia Island	LAT 49°39' LONG 126°34'
Fidalgo Passage	LAT 49°39' LONG 126°34'	Vernaci Island	LAT 49°38' LONG 126°35'
Friendly Cove	LAT 49°36' LONG 126°37'	Williamson Passage	LAT 49°39' LONG 126°23'
Galiano Bay	LAT 49°42' LONG 126°28'	Yuquot Point	LAT 49°35' LONG 126°37
Gold River	LAT 49°41' LONG 126°06'	Zuciarte Channel	LAT 49°38' LONG 126°30'
Gore Island	LAT 49°39' LONG 126°24'		

TOFINO

The west coast of Vancouver Island is a seemingly hopeless confusion of island-cluttered sounds that branch into several long, narrow, tortuous inlets, but of the 5 major sounds, many people consider Clayoquot the most beautiful and awe-inspiring, especially where it is exposed to the open Pacific. There, high swells break into white-capped surf that beats relentlessly against the rugged jumble of islands, rock piles and reefs. It is the type of water usually avoided by prudent boaters, but this is not the case at Clayoquot Sound. Blame it on the fish—chinook, coho and halibut to be precise—that you will find there in good abundance if your timing is right.

Tofino has become the most popular tourist destination on Vancouver Island's west coast, attracting over a million visitors a year. Many go to simply walk the sandy beaches, observe profusions of wading and sea birds, hike along bordering forest trails or challenge the booming breakers with surfboards or kayaks. Other popular activities include offshore boat tours to observe Pacific grey whales on their annual migration north from Baja, California to the Bering and Chukchi seas; sailing, cruising or ocean kayaking the waters surrounding Meares, Vargas and Flores islands; or travelling 65 km northwest by boat or airplane to bathe in the steaming pools of Hot Springs Cove near the mouth of Sidney Inlet.

Tofino, a community of about 2,000 permanent residents, is located on the tip of Esowista Peninsula. It lies at the most westerly point of Highway 4, which winds from the Inland Island Highway at Parksville via Port Alberni to the west coast. Several resorts, hotels and motels offer a full range of accommodations, along with well over a dozen bed and breakfast operations plus hundreds of commercial campsites. However, starting in early March, visitors should make advance reservations for weekends and spring school breaks. By July, reservations are an absolute must, and during August and early September every available type of accommodation is filled to capacity.

There are two public boat-launching ramps in the area. The main ramp, 4th Street Harbour, is located in Tofino, while the Grice Bay ramp is located in Pacific Rim National Park. Moorage can be limited during the peak months of June through August, with the Fisherman's Dock on 4th Street, the Crab Dock on Olsen Road, and Weigh West Marina providing the best options. Method Marine off Main Street has the only

Although the inshore waters of Clayoquot Sound are world famous for salmon fishing, halibut are also found there.

gas dock in town and its marina is used primarily by local residents. Finding parking space for a boat trailer can be challenging so it pays to check for a designated space before you launch.

Although the marine area is well marked with navigation aids, you must watch for hazards like the sand bars off Beck Island, which are exposed at low tide, or Elbow Bank on the west side of Maurus Channel, which has only a foot or so of water over it at low tide. If the water is choppy, a lot of the small floats that mark local crab traps will be barely visible; crab trap lines floating on the surface are also hazardous as they can damage propellers.

For offshore fishing, your boat's navigational equipment should include a marine chart of the area, compass, VHF radio, depth sounder, and a GPS. Although not necessary, a radar unit will certainly help cope with fog. Remember that owning this equipment does little good unless you know how to use it properly. And having a basic knowledge of how to take compass bearings and plot courses on a marine

For visitor information:

TOFINO VISITOR INFO CENTRE
Box 249
1426 Pacific Rim Highway
Tofino, BC, V0R 2Z0
(250) 725-3414
info@tourismtofino.com
www.tourismtofino.com

chart provides good backup should the electronics fail.

The ideal offshore boat is at least 20 feet long with a deep-V hull and a high bow. If using an open boat, expect to get wet. Even moderate winds create a cross-chop on incoming swells, making it impossible to avoid taking in water. Survival suits and rubber boots are an absolute must in order to keep dry and warm. Visitors with their own boats are wise to hire a guide for at least the first day to learn how to get around the area, where to fish and which fishing techniques are productive. This will prove to be money well spent.

Weather and Water Conditions

Despite an annual rainfall that hovers around 125 inches a year, Tofino enjoys the warmest average temperature in Canada. Historical data show that most heavy rains fall during November, December and February. There are stretches of moderate weather in January, March and April, but from then on it is anyone's guess whether there will be rain or sun, and weather swings are usually on short notice.

Visitors planning to fish in May or June should add an extra day or two to their trip as weather insurance. Unsettled weather might be encountered during any typical day but, aside from heavy winds, it is rare to have continuous days where you can't fish offshore. The prevailing westerlies blow at about 25 kmh, which is not a problem for seaworthy boats, but during summer highs most storms are southeasters and they can be nasty.

July and August are bad for fog, which is not a problem for boats outfitted with suitable electronics. Boaters lacking a full range of sophisticated navigational equipment often venture offshore in foggy conditions by buddying up with boats that are properly equipped; however, it is imperative to stay in visual contact throughout the trip.

If you are prone to seasickness, be warned that offshore fishing here involves virtually non-stop up-and-down mixed with persistent side-to-side movement. Swells from the open Pacific are consistent and there is usually a cross-chop. This makes for very uncomfortable fishing, and at times even seasoned sailors turn green. Most store owners in Tofino, knowing

Guide's Tip:

When fishing fresh baits like herring, sardines or mackerel, lightly slash the sides of the bait. This allows the body juices to leak out creating more scent—a very important point for attracting halibut. As in most fisheries, using the freshest bait possible increases your chances.

that anglers will endure almost anything in order to catch fish, carry good stocks of anti-seasick wrist bands, ear patches and non-prescription medications.

Weather permitting, halibut fishing starts about mid-March on the banks offshore from Raphael Point and Portland Point. Most fishing is in less than 150 feet of water, and the bottom is sandy and fairly level. Mooching a cut-plug herring and drift-jigging are the most popular methods, and trolling a cut-plug off a downrigger can be very effective until the dogfish move in around mid-May. Halibut average 20-35 pounds but a fair number run from 50 to 100 pounds and occasionally much larger. By the end of June halibut fishing drops off until fall.

This mixed-bag fishery also yields lingcod up to 40 pounds or more, greenling, some of the largest cabezon (sculpin) found along the BC coast and plenty of rockfish—primarily yelloweye, China, canary, brown, copper, and black. Bottom fishing is also good closer inshore with fair numbers of halibut being caught around Cleland Island.

However, as most anglers are concentrating on inshore coho, the offshore fishing gets very little attention.

Available Marine Charts:

3640 Clayoquot Sound

Marine Chart Coordinates:

Place Names:		Place Names:	
Ahous Point	LAT 49°10' LONG 126°01'	Kutcous Islets	LAT 49°15' LONG 126°04'
Bartlett Island	LAT 49°13' LONG 126°05'	Kutcous Point	LAT 49°15' LONG 126°05'
Blunden Island	LAT 49°11' LONG 126°03'	La Croix Group	LAT 49°09' LONG 126°00'
Burgess Islet	LAT 49°13' LONG 126°02'	Lennard Island	LAT 49°07' LONG 125°55'
"Catface Shoal"	LAT 49°13' LONG 125°58'	Matlset Narrows	LAT 49°14' LONG 125°48'
"Chicken Ranch"	LAT 48°57' LONG 126°01'	Monks Islet	LAT 49°14' LONG 126°01'
Cleland Island	LAT 49°10' LONG 126°05'	Offshore Bank (Rafael Point)	LAT 49°14' LONG 126°14'
Clifford Point	LAT 49°17' LONG 126°02'	Plover Reefs	LAT 49°11' LONG 126°05'
Coomes Bank	LAT 49°13' LONG 126°00'	Portland Point	LAT 49°04' LONG 125°49'
Dawley Passage	LAT 49°09' LONG 125°48'	Rafael Point	LAT 49°17' LONG 126°14'
Duffin Passage	LAT 49°09' LONG 125°55'	Russell Channel	LAT 49°14' LONG 126°06'
Esowista Peninsula	LAT 49°05' LONG 125°50'	"Three Humps"	LAT 49°00' LONG 125°56'
Heisen Bank	LAT 48°54' LONG 125°54'	Tofino Inlet	LAT 49°09' LONG 125°40'
Hobbs Islet	LAT 49°12' LONG 126°02'	Wickaninnish Island	LAT 49°08' LONG 125°56'
Hot Springs Cove	LAT 49°22' LONG 126°16'	Wilf Rock	LAT 49°08' LONG 125°29'
Kennedy River	LAT 49°08' LONG 125°40'		

UCLUELET

This is a great place from which to operate if you plan to fish Barkley Sound or the offshore banks. The sheer abundance of herring, anchovies, needlefish, squid and crustaceans make the area a major year-round feeding ground and, thanks to this dependable food supply, good catches of salmon and bottom fish are possible all year. Ucluelet, population approximately 2,000, is located on the Ucluth Peninsula at the northwestern corner of Barkley Sound. Road access is via Pacific Rim Highway 4, about a 2-hour scenic drive from the new Inland Island Highway junction at Parksville. The peninsula overlooks sweeping, ruggedly beautiful seascapes and surf-pounded shorelines, and the area's abundance and diversity of marine wildlife attracts nature lovers from around the world.

Barkley Sound is also accessible from Bamfield, near its southeast corner, and from Port Alberni, the latter via a 40 km run by boat down Alberni Inlet to the northeastern corner of the sound. It is about the same distance again from there to the outer islands of the Broken Group, the central of the three components of Pacific Rim National Park.

Halibut fishing out of Ucluelet can be a great experience, especially among the islands that dot Barkley Sound.

Weather and Water Conditions

The weather here is typical West Coast—if you don't like it, just wait for five minutes. Winter rains and high winds often shut down offshore fishing for several days at a stretch; spring conditions can be similar only warmer. The summer months are generally good, but as this entire area faces the open Pacific, it is strongly recommended that you keep a sharp weather watch. Starting in August fog becomes a fact of life here.

Even given reasonable conditions, the offshore banks are not for inexperienced or improperly equipped boaters. Those who fish the banks regularly are experienced at locating them, so if using your own boat—assuming it is large enough, seaworthy, and properly equipped—the simplest and safest procedure is to simply follow the recreational fishing fleet out in the morning then stay with them. But it would be a mistake to assume that, if it suddenly turns foggy, you can follow the fleet back for there is no guarantee they will be visible. West Coast weather can be changeable, uncomfortable and—that far offshore—unforgiving. Therefore, in addition to standard safety equipment and foul weather clothing, a well-equipped boat should carry marine charts of the area, a compass and VHF radio. Smaller boats seldom have radar, but a GPS will lead you home should the fog roll in. It will also make relocating the banks easier after the weather clears.

Things to avoid while fishing anywhere off the West Coast. Barkley Sound has its share of rocks and then some.

Norm Reite, the former owner of Island West Resort, probably knows the area's fishing and changeable weather as well as anyone. When asked to offer advice to visitors planning on using their own boats in the area, he replied: "This is a tremendous place to visit and you can have a great time with your own boat—but it's not for the inexperienced. These are exposed waters and there are reefs and rock piles where good fishing is going to draw you in close to them. In order to avoid tragedies, you have to use common sense. That's a major component when you are fishing anywhere but even more so out here. Another point is that if you have just had your boat serviced before coming here, take the time to dump it into your home waters and do your sea trial there. I wish I had a nickel for everyone who has had their boat serviced, then brought it over here and discovered something is screwed up. It happens a lot."

This entire area is noted for excellent catches of halibut, lingcod, and various species of rockfish that include yelloweye, vermilion, yellowtail, China, and sporty black rockfish. Good halibut catches are made offshore around the banks at almost any time but the best fishing is from mid-April until the end of September. A dependable inshore halibut area is located on the north side of Effingham Island, just off the edge of the drop where the bottom levels out.

Spreader bars are the most popular setup, but top-rigged jigs and large drift jigs certainly produce well for those who use them. It's worth noting that whenever El Niño currents swing inland far enough to increase the number of Pacific mackerel in the area, they make excellent halibut bait.

For visitor information:

UCLUELET VISITOR INFO CENTRE
Box 428
2791 Pacific Rim Highway
Ucluelet, BC, V0R 3A0
(250) 726-4600
pacificrimvisitorcentre@telus.net
www.pacificrimvisitor.ca

This chicken fell for a trolled squid hoochie.

Available Marine Charts:

L/C 3602 Approaches to Juan de Fuca Strait
L/C 3603 Ucluelet Inlet to Nootka Sound
3646 Plans—Barkley Sound (Bamfield Inlet, Ucluelet Inlet,
Uchucklesit Inlet, Fatty Basin)
3668 Alberni Inlet (Port Alberni, Robbers Passage)
3670 Broken Group
3671 Barkley Sound

Marine Chart Coordinates:

Place Names:		Place Names:	
Alberni Inlet	LAT 49°05′ LONG 124°50′	Lovett Island	LAT 48°54′ LONG 125°22′
Alley Rock	LAT 48°54′ LONG 125°26′	Mara Rock	LAT 48°53′ LONG 125°29′
Barkley Sound	LAT 48°51′ LONG 125°23′	Mayne Bay	LAT 48°59′ LONG 125°19′
Beg Islands	LAT 48°55′ LONG 125°30′	Meares Bluff	LAT 48°52′ LONG 125°17′
Big (La Pérouse) Bank	LAT 48°45′ LONG 125°55′	Pigot Islets	LAT 48°53′ LONG 125°24′
Boyson Islands	LAT 48°58′ LONG 125°02′	Newcombe Channel	LAT 48°55′ LONG 125°29′
Broken Group	LAT 48°54′ LONG 125°20′	Rainy Bay	LAT 48°58′ LONG 125°02′
Chup Point	LAT 48°57′ LONG 125°02′	"Red Can"	LAT 48°54′ LONG 125°32′
Cree Island	LAT 48°51′ LONG 125°20′	Sail Rock	LAT 48°53′ LONG 125°24′
Drum Rocks	LAT 48°54′ LONG 125°23′	Starlight Reef	LAT 48°53′ LONG 125°29′
Effingham Island	LAT 48°10′ LONG 125°16′	Southwest Corner	LAT 48°50′ LONG 125°49′
Florencia Bay	LAT 48°59′ LONG 125°38′	Swale Rock	LAT 48°55′ LONG 125°13′
Food Islets	LAT 48°55′ LONG 125°29′	Toquart Bay	LAT 49°01′ LONG 125°00′
Forbes Island	LAT 48°57′ LONG 125°25′	Turner Islet	LAT 48°55′ LONG 125°14′
George Fraser Islands	LAT 48°54′ LONG 125°31′	Ucluelet	LAT 48°56′ LONG 125°33′
Great Bear Rock	LAT 48°53′ LONG 125°27′	Ucluelet Inlet	LAT 48°57′ LONG 125°32′
Imperial Eagle Channel	LAT 48°54′ LONG 125°12′	Ucluth Peninsula	LAT 48°57′ LONG 125°35′
La Pérouse Bank	LAT 48°45′ LONG 125°55′	Vernon Bay	LAT 48°59′ LONG 125°09′
Lighthouse Bank	LAT 48°52′ LONG 125°38′	Wreck, The	LAT 48°44′ LONG 125°53′
Long Beach	LAT 49°03′ LONG 125°43′	Wya Point	LAT 48°58′ LONG 125°37′

Guide's Tip:

Leave your rods in the rod holders and
let the wave action work your jigs or
baits. When you get a bite, set the
hook by reeling in rapidly before
pulling the rod from its holder.

Bamfield has some of the most picturesque scenery on the Island's west coast.

BAMFIELD

Visitors to this tiny coastal community have 5 arrival options: the airstrip on the outskirts of East Bamfield; the inlet in which floatplanes land; the MV *Lady Rose*, which sails from Port Alberni each Tuesday, Thursday and Saturday; Western Bus Lines, which operates out of Port Alberni from Monday through Friday; and two gravel logging roads.

The southern route to Bamfield is via Highway 18 from Duncan to Youbou then 85 km of gravel on Central South Main. The eastern route is via Highway 19/19A to the Highway 4 junction; as you enter Port Alberni, take the south Port Alberni turnoff. From there it's about 102 km to Bamfield, including slightly over 80 km of Franklin Main and Sarita Main gravel. Take note that these are active logging roads and expect to meet large trucks, maintenance and service vehicles plus plenty of local traffic. These roads are dusty and in spots extremely rough. Frequent travellers usually carry two spare tires, a precaution that is especially recommended for trailers. If towing a boat, protect everything with tightly fitting covers. Store rods, reels, photographic equipment and clothing in dustproof containers and carry them inside your vehicle.

The Bamfield community is divided in two by Bamfield Inlet. The road ends at East Bamfield, from which point you travel by boat or water taxi to West Bamfield. Each summer the community's population of slightly over 245 swells to well over 1,000 as saltwater anglers, ocean kayakers, canoeists, scuba divers, nature watchers and West Coast Trail hikers swarm into the area. However, there is a good range of accommodations: fishing lodges, a motel with several housekeeping units, rental cottages, bed-and-breakfast operations and campgrounds. If booking into accommodations in West Bamfield, you can make arrangements to be picked up at the government dock there.

The inlet has four government docks, two on each side, but all of them become congested during the summer, and the Bamfield Kingfisher Marina is usually booked a year in advance. Larger boats can be anchored or moored in Bamfield Inlet and Grappler Inlet and at Port Desire. There is an excellent public launch ramp at Port Desire but the adjacent parking area fills to capacity during late July and August. Rental boats are available at Bamfield Kingfisher Marine and there are several independent charter operations.

For visitor information:

BAMFIELD TOURIST/VISITOR INFO BOOTH
General Delivery
Bamfield, BC, V0R 1B0
(250) 728-3006
lmyers@bamfield.ca
www.bamfieldcommunity.com

Anglers with their own boats should consider hiring a guide for at least their initial trip. Offshore fishing requires a large, seaworthy boat equipped with standard safety equipment, marine charts, compass, VHF radio, GPS and, for serious boaters, radar. Having this equiment is of little use, however, unless you know how to operate it. The easiest and safest way to locate the offshore banks is to follow the regulars out in the morning and stay with them. However, if it turns foggy and visibility plummets to near zero, you will require those navigation aids to get safely back to port.

Weather and Water Conditions

Outstanding halibut catches are made around the offshore banks but fishing there is weather controlled. The best period is from mid-April until the end of September but, although summer weather is generally favourable, high swells are simply an open ocean fact of life. Always keep a sharp watch on weather and sea conditions for rapid changes. After the rainy season starts in late September, the weather deteriorates until heavy winter rains and high winds make offshore fishing virtually impossible until after the January halibut closed season. Any fishing that is done happens during the early mornings when the water is calmest.

Expect some fog during the spring fishery and then lots more of it as the weather warms. Fortunately, summer fogs usually burn off by noon.

The most dependable inshore halibut area is Tapaltos Bay, between Whittlestone Point and Lawton Point, but they are also taken around the Bordelais Islets and Folger Island. Most of these halibut are about 15 to 30 pounds, but some up to 150-plus pounds are taken every year. Use top-rigged jigs, large drift jigs or fresh bait on a spreader bar.

You can also expect to encounter lingcod, greenling and cabezon, plus yelloweye, vermilion, yellowtail, brown and China rockfish.

Available Marine Charts:

3671 Barkley Sound
3602 Juan de Fuca Strait, Approaches
3646 Bamfield Inlet
3668 Alberni Inlet
3670 Broken Group

Marine Chart Coordinates:

Place Names:		Place Names:	
Alberni Inlet	LAT 49°05' LONG 124°50'	Hammond Passage	LAT 48°50' LONG 125°14'
Aguilar Point	LAT 48°50' LONG 125°08'	Imperial Eagle Channel	LAT 48°54' LONG 125°12'
Bamfield	LAT 48°50' LONG 125°08'	Kirby Point	LAT 48°51' LONG 125°13'
Bamfield Inlet	LAT 48°49' LONG 125°08'	La Perouse Bank (Big Bank)	LAT 48°45' LONG 125°55'
Barkley Sound	LAT 48°51' LONG 125°23'	Lawton Point	LAT 48°48' LONG 125°11'
Bordelais Islets	LAT 48°49' LONG 125°14'	Leach Islet	LAT 48°50' LONG 125°14'
Boyson Islands	LAT 48°58' LONG 125°02'	Lighthouse Bank	LAT 48°52' LONG 125°38'
Broken Group	LAT 48°54' LONG 125°20'	Pill Point	LAT 48°58' LONG 125°05'
Cape Beale	LAT 48°47' LONG 125°13'	Rainy Bay	LAT 48°58' LONG 125°02'
Chup Point	LAT 48°57' LONG 125°02'	Roquefeuil Bay (Kelp Bay)	LAT 48°52' LONG 125°07'
Cree Island	LAT 48°51' LONG 125°20'	Sandford Island	LAT 48°52' LONG 125°10'
Deer Group	LAT 48°51' LONG 125°11'	Seddall Island	LAT 48°58' LONG 125°04'
Diana Island	LAT 48°51' LONG 125°11'	South Bank	LAT 48°50' LONG 125°49'
Diplock Island	LAT 48°56' LONG 125°07'	Tapaltos Bay	LAT 48°48' LONG 126°11'
Dodger Channel	LAT 48°51' LONG 125°12'	Vernon Bay	LAT 48°59' LONG 125°09'
Edward King Island	LAT 48°50' LONG 125°12'	Weld Island	LAT 48°57' LONG 125°05'
Effingham Island	LAT 48°52' LONG 125°19'	Whittlestone Point	LAT 48°49' LONG 125°11'
Folger Island	LAT 48°50' LONG 125°15'	Wreck, The	LAT 48°44' LONG 125°32'

PORT RENFREW

Port Renfrew is 72 km west of Sooke via Highway 14, a narrow, winding road that reveals some truly scenic ocean vistas. It is a small community but visitors will find several bed and breakfast operations, two motels, a hotel, cabins and three campgrounds with RV parks. The Port Renfrew General Store offers a full line of groceries and is also the community liquor outlet. For dining, check out the Lighthouse Pub and Restaurant and the Port Renfrew Hotel and Pub. If you are interested in a guided trip—which is always recommended for first-timers, even those with their own boats—there are over a dozen fishing charter operators in the area.

If towing your own boat, you will find launch ramps and moorage at the Port Renfrew Marina and the Pacheedaht First Nation Campground and RV Park. The latter is also where the world-famous West Coast Trail begins. Visitors to Port Renfrew can also indulge in ocean kayaking, canoeing on the San Juan River and exploring the world-famous Botanical Beach.

While Port Renfrew is noted for its accessibility to excellent salmon fishing, increasing numbers of anglers appear to be much more interested

Port Renfrew Marina.

The local fleet heading out from Port Renfrew for Swiftsure Bank and some world-class halibut fishing.

in the dependable halibut action that is available, especially offshore around Swiftsure Bank. Inshore halibut fishing can be excellent between February and May when herring migrate to the kelp beds to spawn. Anglers using salmon tackle can combine downrigging or motor mooching for feeder chinooks and halibut, usually with large— 6 to 8 inches long—cut-plug herring. If you are motor mooching along the kelp beds, you will find that 6- to 8-ounce sinkers are usually enough to get down there and make for some interesting times if a barn door takes your offering. This mixed bag inshore action continues until the herring head back out to the offshore banks after spawning.

During the fall some halibut may again be found fairly close to shore, usually off a river mouth where dead salmon are washing downstream. Each year sees halibut taken off the mouths of the Carmanah River and Camper Creek as well as at Nitinat Bar and along the eastern shoreline of San Juan Bay. You can also expect to encounter lingcod— occasionally some huge ones—plus several species of rockfish, cabezon, and various species of flounder.

Weather and Water Conditions

As elsewhere along the Island's west coast there are frequent storms during the autumn, winter and spring and dense fog in the summer. Generally by November the stormy weather makes saltwater fishing

Guide's Tip:

When fishing leadhead jigs with soft plastic tails or bait, attach a short leader with a strong treble hook to the jig hook's shank. This "stinger" will dramatically increase your hookup ratio.

anything from difficult to impossible, so most anglers remain shorebound throughout the winter. But there are occasional calm days during the winter that permit getting out though seldom very far offshore. Prevailing winter winds are usually southeasters.

During the summer, mornings offer the calmest water conditions. Expect fog from June to September though it usually burns off by midday. Low-pressure systems generally result in fairly calm and warm weather, albeit damp, and the prevailing summer winds are usually southwesters.

As the fishing takes place on the open Pacific and often far offshore, a fully-equipped, seaworthy boat is an absolute must, as is experience at boat handling and navigation. The stretch from Port Renfrew to Bamfield is known as the "Graveyard of the Pacific," so it is no place for the ill-equipped or inexperienced. Mistakes or breakdowns can range from scary to fatal as there are few places to go ashore during calm weather and none when it's rough. For this very reason many anglers use the buddy system and head out in groups of two or more boats.

For those using standard halibut outfits, bear in mind that because offshore fishing might call for dropping down deeper than usual—well over 400 feet at places like the Long Hole—loading your reel with braided or monofilament GSP will help detect bites and set the hook more efficiently.

The most popular setup is a spreader bar with a 2-pound sinker and fresh bait on a large circle hook (no. 10/0 to 20/0), but many anglers are now rigging them with soft plastic action baits with built-in scent. Large drift jigs and top-rigged jigs are also used and are almost always sweetened with a piece of fresh bait or scent. And don't overlook large leadheads with soft plastic bodies.

Available Marine Charts:

3602 Approaches to Juan de Fuca Strait
3606 Juan de Fuca
3647 Port San Juan and Nitinat River

Marine Chart Coordinates:

Place Names:		Place Names:	
Bamfield	LAT 48°50' LONG 125°08'	Owen Point	LAT 48°33' LONG 124°30'
Bonilla Point	LAT 48°36' LONG 124°43'	Port Renfrew	LAT 48°33' LONG 124°25'
Botanical Beach	LAT 48°32' LONG 124°26'	Quartertide Rocks	LAT 48°33' LONG 124°28'
Camper Creek	LAT 48°33' LONG 124°33'	San Juan River	LAT 48°34' LONG 124°24'
Carmanah Point	LAT 48°37' LONG 124°45'	Sooke	LAT 48°23' LONG 123°43'
Clo-oose	LAT 48°39' LONG 124°49'	Swiftsure Bank	LAT 48°34' LONG 124°59'
Cerantes Rocks	LAT 48°32' LONG 124°28'	Thrasher Cove	LAT 48°33' LONG 124°28'
Nitinat Narrows	LAT 48°40' LONG 124°51'		

Janice Stefanyk poses with a 32-pound halibut taken while fishing out of Zeballos—the way every fishing trip should end.

INDEX